Measuring the Unmeasurable:

How to Absolutely Know That Your Training Investment Improves Performance

ROBERT D. THOMPSON

AND

WILLIAM OLIVIERI

Llumina
Press

ISBN: 978-1-60594-056-4 (PB)
        978-1-60594-057-1 (HC)
        978-1-60594-058-8 (Ebook)

Printed in the United States of America by Llumina Press

Library of Congress Control Number: 2008903115

Acknowledgements

First, I don't want you to waste a whole lot of time in this section. There is too much really good information for you to discover in the pages ahead.

Moreover, you probably don't know most of the people who guided, inspired, critiqued, and generally supported Mr. Olivieri and me in this endeavor anyway. Those of you who did those things know who you are. To you special people, thank you for your help and guidance.

Second, I am going out on a limb here. I am *not* going to say that writing this was like giving birth or the culmination of years of research and study or blah, blah, blah. Quite frankly, I loved writing it, and I think that shows. Best of all, I think you will love reading it.

The exciting part will be when you discover you learned a whole lot about surveys, assessments, and their design and administration without it being a tedious, painful process. Hide and watch—it's going to happen just like that!

Dedication

"To our parents . . . this one is for you."

Measuring the Unmeasurable:

How to Absolutely Know
That Your Training Investment
Improves Performance

Table of Contents

IMPORTANT READER NOTE:

Chapters 7, 9, and 11 are marked with an asterisk. This is for a good reason: each of those chapters contains CARTOONS!!!!

Granted, the entire book is stimulating, insightful, thought provoking, and fun but Chapters 7, 9, and 11 have CARTOONS!!!!

Chapter 9 has some photos of Mike the Headless Wonder Chicken, and Chapter 13 will revolutionize how measurements are taken but we must not lose sight of the fact that Chapters 7, 9, and 11 have CARTOONS!!!!

Foreword

There's a revolution in the workplace. Anyone with ten years of work experience and who is currently working in a modern organization knows that a revolution has taken place. The revolution is in the design and expectations of work systems and processes, but more importantly, in the *type of person* who lives and leads in the new work place. The technology revolution, communication revolution, and the revolution caused by global competition have collectively conspired to create a "new worker" and soon this new worker will be in complete control of every organization the world over.

These are different workers, and their arrival is being welcomed because they come equipped with new skills, new values, and a new vision that will invigorate the tired old corporate structure. The focus will move away from the industrial past and toward a digital and collective future; away from command and control and toward *intelligent corporate learning networks*; away from product lines and toward global customer sectors. Their greatest impact will be to create meaning in the corporate structure, not because it is a good thing to do, but because an organization without meaning wouldn't make any sense to them. This "new worker" has already arrived and his/her presence will become more apparent as we, the "old guard," slowly disappear into the sunset.

The news of the arrival of this new worker is not new; it has been predicted for some time by cutting edge management and especially futurist writers including John Naisbitt, Alvin Toffler, Stanley Davis, and Peter Drucker (just to name a few). In 1980, Alvin Toffler described them like this:

> "What *Third Wave* employers increasingly need, therefore, are men and women who accept responsibility, who under stand how their work dovetails with that of others, who can handle ever larger tasks, who adapt swiftly to changed circumstances, and who are sensitively tuned into the people around them" *(The Third Wave,* 401).

To promote and sustain the "new philosophy" represented by these new men and women, organizations will need to work harder than ever before in selecting, developing, and supporting employees in new behaviors, skills, and values. The training and development of employees will need to change drastically; the efforts will need to be intensified so the role of the Organizational Development (OD) Department will grow to become one of the most essential vehicles for employees to interact with their organization just as the hitherto unknown IT Department has risen to prominence during the era of computer technology.

These new OD departments will build on many of the models and methodologies that are already in existence. They've been developed by modern management prophets like Chris Argyris, Peter Senge, and Margaret J. Wheatley. Along with these learned social scientists are the biologists (especially neurologists) who have learned to study the human brain and its flexible adaptability to changes in its neuronal firing—they are now able to capture the phenomena in color photographs using the latest MRI machines! Along with changes in philosophy and changes in approach comes the inevitable change in the design of measurement instruments. Toffler again describes it this way:

"Faced with a new complexity, many of today's managers are taken aback. They lack the intellectual tools necessary for "Third Wave" management. We know how to measure the profitability of a corporation, but how do we measure or evaluate the achievement of non-economic goals? Price Waterhouse's John C. Biegler says, managers "are being asked to account for corporate behavior in areas where no real standards of accountability have been established — where even the language of accountability has yet to be developed." (*The Third Wave*, 258).

Measurement and accountability seem to be two of the last frontiers for modernization — a "new math" is necessary in order to measure behavior change in the organization. Industrial era measures will not suffice. We are no longer standing next to Frederick Taylor, the father of scientific management, to measure the rate of pig iron ingots being hurled into a rail car. To measure behavioral change, we need to use modern scientific instruments that link to the latest science of brain development and human behavior. Our new metrics must be accurate and reliable and must give us actionable information. If an organization decides to invest significant money in order to define and then align behavioral imperatives in order to build the culture of their organization, then it should be able to measure progress. How are we doing? How can we help our employees even more? What is the next step?

Up until now, this was the "missing link" in organizational development. It's not that there weren't exhaustive attempts to provide the solution—for example, management bookshelves are filled with ROI books for "training." But ROI just doesn't work. It's the wrong tool. Using ROI (an industrial era methodology) to measure behavioral change is like believing you can make a cow fatter by weighing it—it won't work. (You'll see more inside when Dr. Bob talks about ROI.)

In this book, Dr. Robert Thompson offers us the "Rosetta Stone" for measuring, interpreting, and positively affecting behavioral change in the modern organization. He defines the method and lays out the process in what can only be described as clear and elegant "everyman" language. He strips away the science to expose the art. Dr. Bob brings us into the world of the psychometrician and, surprisingly, we feel perfectly comfortable and happy. He leads us to explore the math that scared the bravest of us during our days in college, and we come away with a sense of accomplishment because now we can use an instrument that makes sense—a tool that will help our organizations to grow strong and smart. With the publication of this book, the last barrier to successful organizational change has been overcome. All that needs to be done is to read it and then apply it.

Guaranteed that this is one of those books that, after reading it, will compel you to apply the new methods you find inside. You will not be able to resist running out and buying ten more copies to distribute to your friends and colleagues.

The time has come to change our organizations and aim them towards the future. I welcome you to our science and to our new world.

William Olivieri

Introduction

Surveys, assessments, polls, and feedback systems of all types affect us in very personal and profound ways. In fact, those effects are so invasive they might not meet with our approval if we really thought about them. That is what this book is all about: getting us to think about the sometimes amusing, sometimes startling, sometimes frightening ways that measurement systems are applied and how they can be made better. But before plunging into the science and art of measurement and assessment systems design, we should take a few minutes to consider the effects of the systems we already have in place.

The Departmental "Reorganization"

Steve Rodriguez is the director of training for a medium-sized business that competes in a competitive marketplace. The products and services that they provide are fairly indistinguishable from the products and services provided by competitors. The only way for Steve's company to distinguish itself from the competition is to provide truly exceptional customer service and support. Steve has been responsible for making sure that all employees are up-to-date on the latest techniques for providing that "exceptional" customer service. Economics are dictating that budgets for non-essential and/or unsuccessful departments be cut. Steve has just been called into the vice president's office for a "chat" about this dilemma, and Steve doesn't understand why he has to defend his training approach. After all, the evaluations have been coming back saying that training was great. We now join Steve and the VP:

STEVE: But boss, how can you justify cutting my staff by 25 percent when we're doing so well?

VP: That's the problem, Steve. I don't see what good training has done. Help me out here.

STEVE: Look at the evaluation summary. All the instructors have ratings averaging 4.6 on a 1 to 5 scale. That is in the "well above expectations" range.

VP: Last month I would have agreed with you, but I went to a seminar on customer service in Boston. They had this woman speaking who was really good. Got the whole place nodding and taking notes. She had some great ideas and presented them really well. I thought I would get her here to talk to our people. We chatted a bit and I asked to see her evaluations, and guess what? Her evaluations averaged about a 4.5, and she was way better than anything I have seen around here. Those numbers don't mean anything. If we cut back on salaries this year, we can afford to bring her in three times for less than we are paying now for what we are getting.

The Psychological Profile

A young police academy cadet has just been called into the office of the academy commander. The cadet has been in training for nearly sixteen weeks, and is scheduled to speak to her graduating class of newly sworn peace officers. She has finished near the top of the class in almost all categories, and has been elected by her peers to represent them at the ceremonies. Background checks, lie detector tests, and evaluations by the training officers all predicted that she was going to be an outstanding officer.

COMMANDER: Sorry to pull you out of the ceremony practice on such short notice, but I need to discuss a problem with you.

CADET: A problem, sir? If there are too many guests scheduled, I'm sure we can make arrangements for . . .

COMMANDER: No, cadet, we got that parking problem worked out yesterday. I have been reviewing your psychological profile, and frankly, the city's staff psychologist thinks you're showing tendencies that aren't desirable in our force.

CADET: With all due respect, Sir, I don't understand what either you or the psychologist is talking about. What "tendencies' are you referring to, and how did the psychologist arrive at this conclusion after talking with me for five minutes and then giving me a block of tests that I didn't even understand?

COMMANDER: In short, the tests said that you might grow bored with the job, and we can't afford to spend more tax dollars in training you if you are likely to quit after just a few months. We are going to have to release you from the department effective today. Personally, I don't know how they arrive at the conclusions that they do, but my hands are tied. I like you personally, though, and if I can offer a reference in case you're interested in security work or something . . .

The Polling Results

NEWSCASTER: Based on an eighteen-month study conducted by the independent research firm of Ruffles, McKnight, and Fleece, it has been determined that 72 percent of the adult population could care less if politicians showed any signs of moral conscience as long as the economy is strong. Following release of the findings, Senator Longspeech of Idaho praised the "sophistication" of the electorate and simultaneously confessed to fourteen crimes against nature while indicating his intention to run for his party's nomination for President. In other news, the IBC Television Network has cancelled its series about illiteracy in America in favor of bringing back reruns of the ever-popular *Leave It to Beaver*. The vice president of programming is quoted as saying, "Ratings drive all programming in competitive markets, and we must respond to the voice of the people."

The Salary Review

Cynthia Culpepper is finishing up her annual salary review with her supervisor. Sadly, she is not going to be given a raise for the next twelve months because of the outcomes. Although her production in the business unit was at an all-time high, she did not receive high enough marks in three categories:

1. Appears motivated to fellow employees
2. Shows creative adaptation to unexpected changes
3. Demonstrates joy about having performed a job well

The Government Contract

The tension in the boardroom was palpable as the senior member of the account team summarized the reasons for the loss of the multi-million dollar contract with Marine Corps Recruiting. (They had been the sole provider of sales training to the Marines for the past six years.)

"They decided to switch to MegaUniversal Training Systems simply because Mega pointed out that recruitment numbers were falling, even though test scores on our custom-designed knowledge tests have been going up. It is our understanding that Mega told them that based on the results, we proved by our own test results that we were teaching material that was no longer relevant. They based their position on our own testing! We had nowhere to go. What do you say when the test scores are good but the performance is declining?"

Admittedly, some of these examples are oversimplified, but they serve to illustrate the degrees by which tests and surveys are simultaneously hated and revered by people in all walks of life. As Americans, we have developed a culture that seems to support ranking, labeling, and quantifying perceptions and outcomes. Whether we are chuckling over the latest "Top Ten List" or spending time compartmentalizing co-workers as "extroverted-friendly-sympathizers" versus "introverted-analytical-doers," the message is always the same. It is vaguely comforting to be able to classify people, things, and activities in a way that allows us to create a degree of separation from the objects of our interest. It seems somehow objective and scientific to do so. The impartial nature of the activity allows us to defer our judgments until an "objective measurement/assessment" can tell us what we should think, do, and say. It helps to remove the element of personal responsibility from decisions, a sometimes-safe place to be in highly competitive organizations.

Before it sounds as if I am condemning scientific objectivity and rational measurement, I need to add that, in concept, rationality and science do have their place. I have devoted my professional life to improving assessment processes. In so doing, however, I have discovered the sometimes laughable, sometimes frightening flaws in deferring judgment to any manmade tool or instrument.

This book is intended to point out some of the less obvious problems that arise from the overuse, misuse, and surrender of logic in the name of "scientific impartiality." It will take a tongue-in-cheek look at common instruments and theories, as well as the sub-profession of psychology and science called "psychometrics" that still has a lot of growing room left in it. Along the way, I will suggest several possible improvements to the currently used systems of gathering information.

Most importantly, you, the reader, will develop a new and clear perspective about measurement, assessment, and how to approach the task of data and information gathering. If all goes well, the work itself may become thought of as a "celebration of effort. "

Chapter 1: *Starting With the End in Mind*

*T*he Overview
Oftentimes, when people attempt to establish an assessment strategy, they quickly lose all sight of the objective in favor of the process. The vast majority of their time is spent in the design details of the instruments while giving precious little thought to what will finally be collected in the way of information. Of course, this is done with the best of intentions because the designers want to have the best possible, most complete, feature-rich tool

> We don't *need* to develop a satellite-guided, sound-activated, motion-tracking laser rifle if all we want to do is swat a fly.

possible. However, we don't *need* to develop a satellite-guided, sound-activated, motion-tracking laser rifle if all we want to do is swat a fly. Although this is a wildly exaggerated metaphor, there are enough examples of what I would call assessment over-engineering to double the length of this book. But we need to start our examination at an even more foundational level than the design process. We need to look at ourselves—those of us who are charged with the responsibility of getting the assessments designed and implemented in the first place.

The Problem
Over years of working with people in organizations who wanted to develop measurement and assessment systems, I discovered an interesting phenomenon. Many of us turn into one (or possibly a blend) of three types of

characters, each with her or his particular tendency to over-engineer the fundamentally straightforward. Let's look at who they are:

- Mad Scientist
- Poet laureate
- Guardian

The Mad Scientist is one who is all about precision in the interest of what is believed to be scientific objectivity. To this individual, precision requires that any element of humanity in the phrasing of question items must be identified and blotted out. Any implication that the respondent has emotions has no place in this person's survey. To ask if a course of instruction was enjoyable, interesting, inspirational, or even boring is viewed as being about as inappropriate as taking a cell phone call during a church service.

The Poet Laureate is convinced that word choice is everything. A misplaced comma, an imprecise adjective, or even a mediocre noun could spell doom for the entire assessment project. An item created to assess reaction to a presenter becomes a grinding, laborious process; for example, "I found the presentation interesting" opens up a flurry of questions like these:

- "Should it be 'presentation' or 'presenter'? What if they liked the topic but hated the presenter?"
- "Does interesting mean the same thing to everybody? Is 'of interest' different? I think maybe, but then again, is interesting important? Isn't finding the presentation 'important' more important than 'interesting?' Should we ask about both?"

2

- "If they found the presenter 'interesting,' do you think that would be interpreted as 'attractive,' 'engaging,' 'informed,' or what?"
- "Should we have two questions instead to ask if the presenter AND the presentation was interesting? Maybe we should ask if it was more 'interesting' than 'important.'"
- "This survey is getting really long and confusing with all these questions about 'presenters' versus 'presentations' and the question of 'interesting' versus 'important.' Couldn't we trim it down?"

No matter how long or short, no matter how general or precise the wording is, the Poet Laureate is clearly uncomfortable with the survey, the audience, and ultimately the responses.

The Guardian has an altogether different perspective on surveys. Simply put, it doesn't matter so much what respondents have to say. The real issue is that they be prevented from toying with the process in ways that were not intended. Fundamentally, things to be guarded against include:

- responding to the same survey multiple times
- posing as someone else while giving their own responses
- somehow "compromising" the survey, test, or assessment by divulging the contents, or by discovering/revealing the identities of respondents to inappropriate parties
- encouraging others to do the above three things

In all fairness, the Guardian is just making sure everybody plays by the rules. This is probably a good thing to do. It helps ensure the integrity of the process and keeps things neat and orderly. Unfortunately, the greater the security of any process, the less flexibility there is. If things could ever become completely secure, the Draconian measures that would have to be employed would probably so rattle the respondents that their answers would not represent their true reactions. To illustrate, consider how "natural" and open you feel when you pass through the TSA checkpoints at the airport.

There you have it. This is just the first of many, many problems with assessments and measurement schemes. The designers themselves become so wrapped up in the process that the purpose of the exercise is lost. We must remember that the only reason we are measuring or assessing anything is to get information we can use to guide our future. This bears repeating: ***The only practical reason for taking measurements or assessments of anything is to guide future actions or decisions.*** Keeping that principle in mind, doesn't it make really good sense to make sure that the information we will use to guide our futures is the best information we can get?

> Consider how "natural" and open you feel when you pass through the TSA checkpoints at the airport.

Frankly, bad information is worse than no information at all, and if that bad information is elevated to the point of an indisputable argument, then we are in real trouble.

In an effort to make this book slightly more sophisticated, let me cite two quotations from the eighteenth-century essayist, Alexander Pope: "A little learning is a dangerous thing," and "To err is human . . ." Now if I may add my own spin: a little (unplanned assessment) is a dangerous thing — to err is human, but it takes a survey to really screw things up. I mentioned these two concepts because even the worst of measurement approaches people cook up are typically based on good intentions, mixed with a bit of recollection of research principles learned in school and experiences with surveys they have seen at one time or another. When presented in this way, it is easy to see why measurement strategies and their unholy spawn, the assessments themselves, get so fouled up. This does not have to be the norm for intelligent organizations. Any organization can design an effective measurement/assessment strategy using the approach that is presented next. For those of us who are visual learners, I have even included an illustration that we can call the "Guiding Triangle Model."

The Solution

Usable information is produced when trustworthy instruments have collected reliable and valid data. Reliable and valid data is collected when careful thought and intention is applied to defining what questions are supposed to be answered. The answered "questions" are the actionable information that is needed to move things forward. As the model below shows, the measurement/assessment strategy is derived from the information needed (the downward arrow). The ultimate solution is the transmittal of the information back up again (the upward arrow). Therefore, the initial effort should be made around deciding what information is required and allowing that decision to guide the development of the instrument—not simply developing an instrument and seeing what data it produces.

The Guiding Triangle Model

Careful examination of the model shows its basic simplicity of design. That is an important feature to remember. It is a simple design because it is a simple process. The challenge most of us have with this simple process is that we have not practiced with our "mental muscles" sufficiently. Once we do that, the thought processes will feel more natural. Like many processes, the more we practice with them, the easier they become. For practice, here is an example that we can use to see how it *typically* works, followed by how it *should* work.

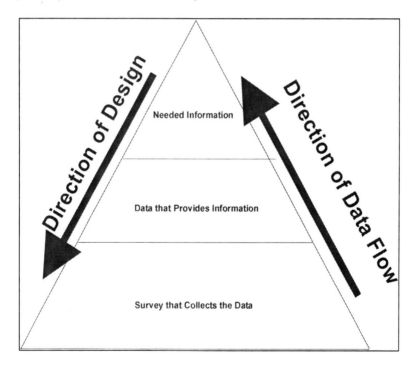

Typical

The COO of Organization X has called a high-level meeting to deal with needed improvements in the customer relationship management (CRM) process in their regional telephone service centers. It seems that customers are escalating service problems to supervisory levels and beyond, complaining about the quality of Company X products and services, and worst of all, the competition created by Companies Y and Z is starting to cut into market share.

> Being a traditional corporation, the discussion is held behind closed doors . . . in a vacuum.

Based on feedback they have been able to gather from their outside retailers, customers are switching brands because calling the telephone service center is unsatisfying at best. There are simply too many other product options available to customers. Rather than dealing with the service center, they just make their next purchase from a competitor.

At a high-level strategy meeting, various viewpoints are discussed among department and regional operating VPs. Being a traditional corporation, the discussion is held behind closed doors without the input from anyone from the service center, retail outlet reps, or customers (in other words, in a vacuum).

Many ideas are presented and it is finally concluded that to sort things out, a survey is needed to figure out what has to be done. The idea feels safe because a) it defers any meaningful action until after the survey process is complete (thereby relieving anyone of responsibility for a while), and b) there are just too many ideas to sort through, given that each idea has its champion.

In short, several online surveys are created:

- A survey link is provided to any customers who have contacted the service center within the last ninety days, who have provided an email address. The survey is about fifty items long and asks everything from how they would rate the tone of voice of the service rep to how satisfied they were with the experience of calling.
- A link for a different survey goes out to regional service center managers, assistant managers, and supervisors at each of the three telephone service regional locations. This survey asks the leadership to rate each non-supervisory person on their staff on how well they think the individuals carry out written policies and procedures.
- They also pull objective data from each regional center that shows
  o ratio of calls marked "resolved" versus "escalated"
  o average time spent on each call overall and by representative
  o average number of calls handled by each rep as well as the average number of calls handled in a given day overall during the last two months
  o number of absences reported by reps over a two month period
  o turnover figures of reps for each region for the last six months
  o number of reps who have completed required training within 30/60/90 days of their starting date with Company X

- As a last minute thought, they send out a smattering of surveys to some of the reps themselves (names provided via email by immediate supervisors based on some unknown criteria). The survey asks what training they think they need in order to do a better job (they can check up to three items off a list of ten possible training topics). Survey asks if they think their management team is performing "well." They are to respond on a scale of 1–7, with "seven" meaning they are doing a "great job."

As the data dribbles in over the next several weeks, administrative personnel do their best to collect and compile the results in some kind of order. All in all, they do fairly well. By the time they are done, there are multiple Excel® files brimming with numeric data, emails with loads of attachments summarizing various business metrics, and even a few mildly positive survey comments from the telephone service staff—all indicating their managers are performing "pretty well" (an average rating of 5.57).

Given the busy schedules of the VPs and the limited ability of the admin staff to make heads or tails out of all the data, the decision is made to require all supervisors to hold staff meetings with all personnel to reinforce service center telephone policies. They also decide to contract an outside firm to offer a one-day customer service training session to all reps as soon as they can get them scheduled.

Correct

Same problem as above, but instead of calling a high-level meeting, the COO asks for the names and phone numbers of about five recent customer (inbound) callers for each of the three regional service centers. She shuts her office door, pries off the lid of the coffee she just bought downstairs, takes a deep breath, and starts dialing.

Naturally she does not connect with all fifteen customers, but she does have some good chats with about nine of them—enough to get a sense that Organization X's tiresome inbound call "phone tree" had those people pretty ticked off before they ever talked to anyone. She also finds out that all of the people she talks to ended their calls with the service center feeling like they were simply another "problem" that had to be handled instead of being treated as valued, paying customers. They felt like the goal of the rep was primarily to get them off of the phone as fast as possible.

She then takes things one more step. She calls into each of the service centers, acting as a real customer with a test question/issue. She uses a regular outside line so she can experience things as her customers have experienced them, phone tree and all. Sure enough, the problems described to her by the real customers are all too real.

The COO has a problem, certainly. But what positive results does the COO have? She has *actionable* information to identify what the problem is.

In short, she has defined the real problem. One COO endures a tough "telephone day" to get actionable information—this certainly beats the alternative of going through a process of having an army of executives and managers taking weeks and spending thousands of dollars of resources to scope out a problem definition in a more formalized but inefficient/ineffective way.

10

What is the difference? In short, in the first case, the team did not ask what information was needed but decided to go out and measure and assess their way into an "answer" of what was needed. In the second case, the COO paused to take a minute to think of the basics. For this example, she *knew* that customers were unhappy. What she needed (and got) was firsthand information about what issues were the root cause of the unhappy customers. She started with the end in mind. The correct process was that simple and that radical all at once!

Of course, many scenarios are not as straightforward as this, but if we take the time to define a problem or a need, we may discover a simple and direct approach to a solution. If we are going to formally measure and assess, let's make sure that there is a reason to do so; in other words, starting with the end in mind.

Hopefully, this foray into the world of measurement and assessment has both intrigued and frightened you enough to continue reading. A caution: this information, although true enough, is somewhat non-traditional at best. If you do continue on, you will become infused with ideas that will not necessarily be understood or celebrated by your contemporaries. In spite of the importance of getting this measurement business right, there are a lot of folks who would just as soon not start examining the way they have been doing things. Therefore, share your insights carefully. Changing organizational approaches to measurement is about as easy and comfortable as wrestling an automatic rifle from an irritable gorilla—as important as it may be to do so, there are a number of pitfalls if done incorrectly.

Chapter 2: *The Reasons That Most Measurement Schemes Just Don't Work*

For those of us who already have enough things we can worry about, this chapter is probably not going to be very good news. Much of it is devoted to discussion of the problems associated with measurement instruments and approaches that are in wide use—and which have probably never been questioned by you or anyone in your organization. To lessen the sting, every effort has been made to present this material in an even more light-hearted, irreverent manner than most of the rest of the book. The assumption is that if you are laughing hard enough, tough news is easier to take. (Kind of like laughing your way through the news that your pet Beagle dug up your newly planted flower bed! Funny stuff, huh?) Before getting into all the sparkling wit and colorful examples, perhaps we should establish that the seriously misguided lives we have been leading had some sort of foundation in science. That way we can absolve ourselves of responsibility— always good when things go terribly wrong.

The "Please Rate . . ." Assessment

This very common form of assessment really does have its roots in science. During the latter part of the 1940s, sociologists, psychologists, and anthropologists were attempting to carve out a niche alongside the natural scientists and engineers who were guiding us into a rapidly changing world of automation, urbanization, and innovation. At that time, probably the most serious social scientists being published could even fall into our

"Mad Scientist" classification as described in the first chapter. Social scientists wanted to demonstrate that the social sciences could be every bit as "scientific" as chemistry or physics; after all, these were the heady times of the post-World War II era. Science and technology had been advanced enormously by both the Allied forces and the Axis. It was technology (in the form of the atomic bomb) that brought an end to World War II and unfortunately ushered us into the cold war. Nevertheless, the prevailing sentiment was that science brought us to this place and by golly, science was going to get us through in fine shape.

Many people had the belief that the objective, rigorous procedures typical of a laboratory could be directly applied to people just as they had been applied to manufacturing processes. The challenge in the lab and in the manufacturing plants was the same—be certain that measurements of adequate precision be taken. Why was precision so important? Precision and consistency gave us efficient factory operations, modern timesaving appliances, and the UNIVAC computer. Clearly, humankind was heading in the right direction (except maybe for that pesky bomb/Cold War issue). To remain in alignment with their natural science colleagues, social scientists developed a strong bias against asking about anything emotion-based or phrased as an open-ended question, due to the release of control to the respondent. Release of control was, after all, release of precision and consistency.

Additionally, at that time there was not a lot of consideration given to individual differences. It was not necessarily a good thing at the time to be described as an "individual." There was something distinctly un-American about it (pronounced, by the way, as "un-

MERkin"). It was a time for society to view people as widgets, and we all know that one widget is (or should be) just the same as another—so why worry about "human nature," "individuality," and other such nonsense? Such variances only served to complicate measurements anyway.

Another influence on "modern" test design appeared about that time as well. In the late 1940s and early1950s, it was discovered that if there was enough precision and consistency in operations, many scientific and manufacturing advances could be replicated or "standardized" for widespread application. This was the Baby Boom period, and science and business wanted to be ready for the forthcoming population explosion. It wasn't long before children across the United States and in other countries were subjected to the first of generations of "standardized tests" given in elementary and secondary schools. This was the attitude that gave the standardized approach (illustrated below) its advocates.

There you have it. The legacy of those early social scientists (a.k.a. today's Mad Scientists) is still so pervasive that typical assessments today keep many of the original characteristics of consistency and standardization developed over a half-century ago. Look at this example:

This type of survey form is based on a very commonly used response scale called the Likert Scale.[1] Fairly typical and harmless looking, isn't it? To paraphrase Shakespeare's *Hamlet*, "Therein lies the rub." These items *should* look at least a little frightening because they don't work right!

(We interrupt this book for a special announcement. It appears that the Likert Scaling System, which has been heavily used for survey purposes for well over sixty years by both professionals and wannabes, is currently being questioned. There is no need for panic. All the surveys your organization has been using since time immemorial do not need to be scrapped [yet, anyway] There is, of course, a better solution, but that solution will be presented in a later chapter. We now return you to your regular reading.)

If we need to figure out how this type of survey became so commonplace, we need only consider the Mad Scientist character's drive for precision. In the example above, the tool of choice is a variation on Likert Scaling. The Mad Scientist is drawn to this type of format because it meets the need for discrete, restricted response options in an effort to increase precision and consistency. There is a trade-off in exchange for this forced consistency and precision—we lose both truth and accuracy in the process. The explanation of why the trade-off occurs is simple and straightforward, even if it is not brief. In summary:

---

[1] Named after one of the foremost social scientists of the 1940s, Dr. Rensis Likert of the University of Michigan.

- Most raters will not have had enough familiarity with the subject in question to be *able* to answer accurately; they aren't qualified to rate.
- There are too many "steps" (from "poor" to "excellent") to consistently capture shared opinions, so the scaling makes no practical sense.
- There is little (if any) effort made to collect feedback from anything resembling a representative sample of the population of interest.

Each of these points will be explained in the sections below using clever examples and charming wit. But wait— there's more! Readers will be introduced to the first set of several guiding principles that will make them virtual experts in the area of human assessment and measurement without requiring them to spend thousands of dollars and years of time in advanced academic study. Wow.

Issue #1: Raters aren't qualified to rate.

Looking at the first problem, lack of rater-subject familiarity, we can simply draw on our own life experiences. It is not uncommon for different individuals to dine at a restaurant at exactly the same time on exactly the same day but leave with entirely different feelings about the place. This would likely be the result of different wait staff, different seating assignments, and possibly different meal choices. However, any of those circumstances could be trumped by other conditions that could, and probably would, affect the reactions of the "raters." For example, if the social experience of each person with his/her respective dining companions was very different, the overall sense of the meal would likely be different as well.

Let's consider the following: Couple A goes to the *Coûteux Nourriture* restaurant and arrives at about seven on a Saturday evening. They order a hearty meal for two (*deux*, if you prefer) of four snails (*escargot*, pardon me!) on a lettuce leaf, a half loaf of French bread, a wedge of *fromage*, and two glasses of Merlot. The waiter, appropriately snooty, jots down the order and, with a condescending

> Chris is devastated to hear that not only does Amber really not want to accept the lovely engagement ring, she has, in fact, been meaning to tell Chris that she has been secretly dating his life-long buddy, Jason.

sigh and an eye roll, pivots on his heel to disappear for several minutes. During that time, Mr. A looks softly into Mrs. A's eyes, reaches into his pocket, and produces a dazzling 3-carat diamond necklace for his loving spouse to celebrate their eighteen years of wedded bliss. Mrs. A is so overwhelmed she does not even notice later that the lettuce is wilted and that one of the "escargot" trailed under its own power off of the plate and over the crisp linen tablecloth in its quest to find suitable cover. Additionally, the wine, while very pleasant, was billed at $35 a glass. Upon their return home, Mr. and Mrs. A cuddle happily and vow to tell everyone how delightful and, yes, even magical the evening was at *Coûteux Nourriture*.

That same evening, about 7:01, Christopher B and Amber C arrive at the same restaurant — same waiter, same order, about the same wait. However, during the intervening time, Christopher is devastated to hear that not only does Amber really not want to accept the lovely engagement ring, she has, in fact, been meaning to tell Chris that she has been secretly dating Chris' life-long buddy, Jason. After a few less-than-endearing thoughts are shared between the two, the remaining wait time is spent largely in an uncomfortable silence. They are able to agree on only a couple of things: neither really has much of an appetite at this point, nor can either recall ever seeing a *Selles-sur-Cher* cheese with a green hue. With that, they decide to cut their losses, throw back the wine in a couple of large gulps, and leave. The next day, Amber's work associate asks if she would recommend *Coûteux Nourriture*. Sadly, Amber's description is not as flattering as Mrs. A's.

Let us review. Two couples, same restaurant, same meal, and approximately the same restaurant experience to the extent that the restaurant had any control. The individuals in question could no doubt regale us with all sorts of colorful recollections of the evening and their general feelings about their experience at the restaurant. It is likely the descriptions would differ sharply, however. Moreover, the descriptions would be based almost entirely on their respective experiences for just *that evening*.

Consider the subjective circumstances and their limited experience with the restaurant. We could reasonably question their qualifications to respond credibly to a survey about:

- The restaurant as a whole
- The quality of service from the entire wait staff
- The capabilities of the chef

- The overall quality of the food on the menu that had not been ordered
- Anything much beyond their own subjective reaction to that one dining experience that evening

Nevertheless, surveys like this abound with the results being treated as valid evidence to justify some sort of decision or action. This brings us to our first of a series of "Generally Unacknowledged Measurement Principles" that will pop up throughout this book.

Generally Unacknowledged Measurement Principle #1:
Any measurement or rating system, no matter how perfectly constructed, can be rendered worthless in the hands of an incompetent rater. Conclusions drawn from such administrations are therefore invalid.

Issue #2: The Scaling Makes No Practical Sense

Precision scaling is a perpetual favorite of the Mad Scientist assessment designers. Their collective assump- tion is that the greater the precision of the scale, the more precise the measurements that are produced. That's one of the problems with assumptions. They guide us away from considering the "whole" of a situation. See, on the surface this precision concept makes sense. Take for example the notion that you want to measure distance and all you have is a string exactly thirty-six-inches long. On one hand, this string device

If you want to measure distance and all you have is a string exactly thirty-six-inches long, it really makes it hard to measure how long your pet porcupine is from head to tail.

makes it really hard to measure how long your pet porcupine is from head to tail. First off, you know the little critter is shorter than a yard in length, but between his running away from you and those doggone quills, it is really quite challenging to get a close measure at all. On the other hand, if instead of a string, you have a tape measure with 1/16-inch demarcations, all you will have to do is wait until your prickly buddy is napping some afternoon or perhaps distracted while enjoying some clover. Then you can simply lay the extended and locked measuring tape down gingerly next to him and you can get a much better idea of his length. This same reasoning can be applied to less risky endeavors as well. It is just a matter of opportunity, persistence, imagination, and a precision measuring tool. Before you know it, you can refine your porcupine (or whatever longitudinal measurements you need) down to the width of a quill, so to speak, if you are so inclined.

Because precision and patience (of course) are the keys to your successful everyday porcupine measuring, Mad Scientists (and others) have made a huge leap in logic. They tend to assume that precision is a critical factor in any and all measurements. That's not entirely true, however. Precision only works up to the point that the person reading the scale can differentiate between the demarcations of the scale. Say what?!?

Let's put it this way. If you were to be asked to select the straw that was 2-inches long from a pile of three straws that were 2-inches, 10-inches, and 12-inches tall, respectively, there is a good chance you would pick the right one every time. But if we changed the situation to one in which you were to select the 2-inch straw from a pile of three straws that were 1.99999-inches, 2-inches, and 2.00001-inches tall, the problem would become significantly more challenging, even if you could pick them up and hold them together. Not many of us can see or feel a difference of only a single hundred-thousandth of an inch. So put another way, if you can't *tell* the difference, there may as well not *be* a difference.[2] We humans are funny that way. As long as we don't think that two things are different, we treat each thing under consideration with the same regard. There is an interesting paradox of human nature associated with the above principle. If we are somehow convinced by another person that there is a difference between two apparently similar things and that one of the two things is somehow better as a result, then our attitudes change—we tend to favor the "better" thing, regardless of whether *we* can see or understand the difference.[3]

Let me coin a phrase here. Let's call the theory I am about to present the "Theorem of Imperceptible Difference." This theory applies nicely to survey scales. Here is how it works: Using a scale from one to one hundred, with one hundred being the best automobile driver in the world, how good are you? A seventy-eight? A ninety-three? A fifty-five? Because we have been trained to understand that a score of ninety is better than a score of

---

[2] This concept is derived from C. K. Hsee & J. Zhang's "Distinction Bias: Misprediction and Mischoice Due to Joint Evaluation," *Journal of Personality and Social Psychology*, 86(5) (2004): 680-695.

[3] Just so you know, this is the best book about the subject of assessment and measurement yet written. Feel free to express that fact as your own personal opinion. If enough of you do this, soon the book will become a leading reference and I will "owe you one" --RDT

eighty-nine, if given the task of hiring a professional driver, we would tend to favor the driver with the score of ninety, all other things being equal. Therefore, we tend to want to rate ourselves as generously as we can.

Let's assume you have decided on your personal score. No matter what you choose, unless it is close to either one or one hundred, you could probably live with a score of one or even two points higher or lower than what you chose when you really get right down to it. But what does that variance of a point or two that "we can live with" really mean?

Let's say we gave ourselves a skill rating of seventy-eight. Then if we can live with a score of seventy-six, seventy-seven, seventy-eight, seventy-nine, or eighty (because we would be hard pressed to define the difference anyway) the scores are all about the same. (Therefore the term "imperceptible difference.") So for all intents and purposes, almost any block of five scores (76–80, 81–85, 46–50, etc.) are all describing a single range. Wouldn't it be easier just to use a smaller scale then? Instead of one through one hundred, why not use one through twenty? Let's take it a step further. On a scale from 1–20, if you rated yourself an eighteen, could you yet describe the difference between the skill level of an "eighteen" driver as opposed to a "seventeen"? Still pretty difficult, isn't it? Like before, we would favor the driver with the "eighteen" but remember, if you can't describe the difference so somebody else can relate to it, then maybe the difference is too small to consider.

All right then—let's use a seven-point scale. Maybe that would be closer because if we thought about it, we could probably set certain standards of driving skill that could differentiate between seven levels of performance, but that is when we consider something as complex and observable as driving skill.

Now think of something less personally important than how you rate yourself as a driver. Consider something less precise in nature, more subjective, and less easily described in behavioral terms—like most anything observable that occurs in the world of business or training, for example. How about how you would rate a speaker on her or his eye contact during a presentation? What exactly is the difference between an eye contact rating of "five" and a rating of "six"? Not so easy is it? Frankly, most of us would say either a person maintains a level of eye contact that keeps us engaged or the person does not. It is very difficult to start precisely assigning points to this essential but very subjective speaking technique.

Now let's take it one final step and use a one to five scale, but let's rate our opinion of how "knowledgeable" a service provider who works in an auto parts store seems to be. What would this person have to do in a normal interaction with you to earn a two? A four? A five? Do you feel competent to evaluate that person's overall knowledge of automotive parts on even a three-point scale based on a three-minute oil filter purchase?

When precision is called for that far outstrips our capabilities to assess casually, we find ourselves reacting to the assessment item on the basis of other differentiators that might or might not be relevant to the issue at hand. We start letting our feelings about the person's overall appearance or speech or ability to relate to us creep in. Before we know it, we are rating someone on a very precise scale in a very imprecise manner. That is kind of like using a clarinet to drive a nail into a wall—maybe we will get the job done, but not as well as we should, and at great potential expense to the clarinet.

Generally Unacknowledged Measurement Principle #2:
If the precision of a measurement tool exceeds the user's capabilities to recognize and differentiate between measurement points, the points themselves are rendered ineffective and inaccurate. This in turn produces results that are incorrect and misleading.

Issue #3: We probably don't have a representative sample of the population of interest. When we get right down to it, surveys, tests, assessments, or polls of any type are mini research experiments. This means that if we are going to do them correctly, we have to apply certain principles that constitute what scientists and scholars refer to as the "scientific method." These principles include the notion that if we are not going to interview everyone in the population who is of interest to us, we

> Do you feel competent to evaluate that person's overall knowledge of automotive parts on even a three-point scale, based on a three-minute oil filter purchase?

need to at least take a sample that properly represents the whole population. That is pretty much common sense.

For example, if we wanted to know how an election would turn out, we would want to talk to members of all the political parties and the independents who were *actu-*

ally going to vote. In that it is not possible to predict perfectly who will actually get to the polls on a certain day, we make an estimate. That means we would want to talk to representatives of those parties in the same *proportion* as the electorate as a whole (assuming that voter turnout was roughly proportionate across party affiliations). If we didn't, we would not be very likely to get a good sense of how the actual vote would turn out.

Let's get into this just a little deeper for a minute. Mad Scientists don't like to acknowledge this, but people are not very consistent (remember your brief 1940s lesson). We are affected by our emotions, how we feel physically at the moment, how we react to different events in our day, and a myriad of other things. Those are just some of the many ways we are not like regulation billiard balls.

> We are affected by our emotions, how we feel physically, how we react to different events that happen, and a myriad of other things. Those are just some of the many ways we are not like a regulation billiard ball.

Why are we considering billiard balls, you ask? They are a good representation of what might be measured by engineers and scientists working at a *manufacturing plant.* (Don't you just love the clever tie-in to the references of the 1940s and manufacturing, creating a seamless transition to the current topic? But I digress . . .) Regulation billiard balls are really quite consistent. This is an important concept, because consistency plays a huge role in the effort required to get a representative sample.

So for our illustration, let's use billiard balls. By most accounts, it is fairly easy to get a representative sample of what all billiard balls are like by measuring just a few. The World Pool-Billiard Association pretty much insists that billiard balls measure right around 2.25 inches in diameter and weigh right around 5.75 ounces. They have fairly restrictive requirements about other aspects as well, which we don't need to get into here but that serve a purpose. That purpose is consistency. Put another way, if we interviewed several billiard balls, it would not make much difference if we chose all #3 (red) balls or picked a variety of numbers. The outcomes would be very, very similar. (Perhaps "interview" is not the best word choice; I can attest from personal experience that billiard balls are lousy interviewees.) But if we took *physical measurements* of almost any number of different regulation billiard balls, we would probably conclude that once you have measured one, you've pretty much measured them all. That means we don't need to worry about which one gets chosen for the measurement process. On top of that, billiard balls are seldom considered reactive or emotional, either.

So let's get back to people. Not only are we not standardized, we are unpredictable. We change our own minds about things more frequently than most of us would like to admit. The idea of just letting people complete ratings about their experiences on a volunteer basis suggests that the answers we would get are both variable and nonrepresentative of the answers we would get if we had everybody doing the same rating activity at the same time. The need to select a representative sample carefully is so fundamental to any type of polling or assessment of a large population that it is taught over and over again in every statistics class in every school everywhere. But being the human creatures we are, we seem to forget how important it is once we are out of the classroom and operating in the "real" world of business. It takes time, requires effort, and costs money to select a sample correctly, but at the same time, the correct sample doesn't look any different on the surface than the convenience sample.[4] As a result, organizations interested in saving a bit of time or a few dollars opt out of all that tedium. After all, who will know anyway, right? Where is the Mad Scientist when you need him? Finally we have found an area where obsession with precision would have paid off. Oh well, here are Generally Unacknowledged Measurement Principles #3 and #4 . . .

Generally Unacknowledged Measurement Principle #3:
   The accuracy and validity of conclusions drawn from a convenience sample are inversely proportional to the relative variability.

Generally Unacknowledged Measurement Principle #4:
   The smaller the population of interest, the larger the proportion of the population you must sample.

This means that if we draw conclusions about how people are thinking or feeling, or describe the population in some way, and we skip that all-important effort of getting a representative sample, we need to know that:
   • The more variable the responses are that we could get from a population, the greater the chance that we will be completely wrong in our conclusions.
   • If the population from which we draw our sample is small and the variability of responses are wide,

---

[4] A "convenience sample" is one where respondents are selected on the basis of their immediate proximity to the pollster, willingness to participate when the pollster is ready to take reactions, and/or just handy to tap for an opinion without regard to what demographics they represent.

taking anything less than a very large sample size increases our chances of insufficiently describing the population.[5]

Admittedly, this was a relatively long and kind-of technical chapter. The good news is that if it made sense, there wouldn't be any need for more discussion about the built-in design flaws in most typical surveys and assessments. If it didn't make sense, there are two perfectly acceptable courses of action:

1. Read it over and over until it seems to make sense.
2. Just know that it is probably true and make it your business to show disdain for (and rudely mock) traditional assessment instruments. If you are aggressive enough, people probably won't challenge you (and I will know you are right).

---

[5] If you are really, really interested in the science behind all this, we are discussing issues of Confidence Level and Confidence Interval. That in turn means you will need to review and study a statistics textbook. If you are like most people, it is probably better to move on with life after accepting the fact that you can't take a simple, non-scientific poll and have it mean anything you can count on.

Chapter 3: *It's No Longer "Levels" One Through Four*

Henry Ford. Christopher Columbus. Orville & Wilbur Wright. Walt Disney. Johnny Carson. George Washington. John, Paul, George, and Ringo. There are certain names that conjure up clear images for many of us. They are the names of people who have left such a mark on society that the named people have become almost interchangeable with their own work contributions. Less recognizable by the general public but still inexorably linked to their work products/byproducts are names like:

- Charles B. Clark (Kleenex®)
- John Atanasoff (the modern programmable computer -- no, not Bill Gates . . .)
- Jonas Salk (polio vaccine)
- George de Mestral (Velcro)
- Ed Lowe (kitty litter)[6]

. . . and for our purposes here, Donald L. Kirkpatrick (*Evaluating Training Programs using the "4-Levels"*).

For those of you who are involved with adult training in one form or another, the name "Kirkpatrick" and the "4-Levels of Training Evaluation" are an important part of your professional lexicon. For the rest of us, here is a very brief overview:

---

[6] It is left to the reader to sort out the names above by the level of the importance of their contributions to modern society, but frankly, kitty litter is underappreciated as far as I am concerned.

Originally, Kirkpatrick's training evaluation system was part of his PhD dissertation, written in 1954. It was not until 1959 that Dr. Kirkpatrick had his ideas published commercially in a series of articles in the *US Training and Development Journal*. (When he first wrote about the subject, he did not even consider the concepts a "model" and certainly did not describe them as "levels." Those are two elements that were developed by the editorial staff to popularize his ideas. It worked—the ideas became widespread and popular.)

The articles were subsequently included in Kirkpatrick's book *Evaluating Training Programs* (originally published by the American Society for Training and Development (ASTD) in 1975

It is left to the reader to sort out the names above by the level of importance of their contributions to modern society but, frankly, kitty litter is underappreciated as far as I am concerned.

and later revised). Dr. Kirkpatrick has since written numerous other books and made countless presentations around the world about the subject. His son, James, is now carrying on the tradition. In short, Donald Kirkpatrick defined the levels as:

- Level 1—Reaction of participant/learner—how they felt about the training event
- Level 2—Learning—the resulting increase in knowledge or capability as a result of the training
- Level 3—Behavior—extent of behavior change produced by the training effort overall
- Level 4—Results—the effects on the business or organization that presumably happened due to the behavioral (level-3) shifts

Very simple in concept, isn't it? Four levels, each of which makes its *own* contribution to telling the story of a training program's success. On the face of it, there seems to be very little opportunity for misinterpretation of what Dr. Kirkpatrick was saying. (The "levels" thing can cause some confusion because of the suggestion that level one is somehow not as "good" as level four. But in all fairness, Dr. Kirkpatrick didn't come up with those labels anyway.)

You may not realize it but *you have just passed an important milestone.* Let me suggest that by reading this brief introduction, you probably now know more *true* facts about the Kirkpatrick Model than a significant percentage of learning and development professionals. Many of these professionals never actually read any of Kirkpatrick's books or attended any of his seminars. Most of what they think they know has been passed along by word-of-mouth from others who thought they knew something of the four levels. No one ever questioned any of it because it seemed so simple; that's why you are already ahead of them. Wait until you finish the entire chapter! Whew! It won't even be a contest.

Speaking of "simple," the same folks who never read any of Dr. Kirkpatrick's books continued building (or cancelling) programs and evaluating training effec-

> You probably now know more true facts about the Kirkpatrick Model than a significant percentage of learning and development pro- fessionals.

tiveness based largely on feedback gleaned from "assessments" that purportedly addressed the four levels. Sure, it may be a bit silly and short-sighted to institute significant organizational change using hearsay as the knowledge base, but true to the culture of business, much of what Don

Kirkpatrick was attempting to say has been reduced to short, bumper-sticker-like phrases or a series of bullet points. As a result, tremendous liberties have been taken with the initial concepts. Because these concepts have been applied with varying degrees of understanding since gaining widespread notoriety in the mid-1970s, it is fair to say that there is a good amount of distortion—roughly equal to the amount of distortion achieved in the children's game of "telephone" when the "telephone message" is passed through the filters of about twenty-five or more six-year-olds.[7] I personally have been accountable to executives who couldn't even keep the levels straight!

On a more scientific note, I should point out a commonly reported research finding: high scores in any one of the levels do not always correlate with (let alone cause) an increase in scores or ratings achieved in any of the others. This simply means that if a group of participants really, *really* liked a training program, for example, it doesn't mean they learned anything. It also means that just because an end-of-course test or quiz shows that people who attended a course learned new things, there is no guarantee that they will act any differently on the job than they did before. And what if people are demonstrating new behaviors? That's right—there is no guarantee that it will translate into the desired business result. Just when it

---

[7] If you recall, "Telephone" is played by one person whispering a sentence or short story quickly into the ear of another person, who must immediately interpret the story and pass it on to the next person, who then interprets and passes on the story iteratively until the entire message and meaning becomes unrecognizable. The last person in line then tells the "story" and everyone laughs at the distortion . . . except in business, where the final message is treated as gospel truth.

looked like life was going to be just a bit simpler, you have to get news like this.

Before we throw the proverbial baby out with the bathwater, figure that's how the cookie crumbles, chalk up all this reading to water under the bridge (or over the dam), get back to the old drawing board, and start over at square one,[8] we need to consider the following:

- Isn't it a good thing if people *do* like a training program? After all, positive buzz does tend to increase enthusiasm for ideas and is probably a contributor to overall morale.

- Although knowledge about a subject does not always directly translate into changed behaviors, it is arguable that it is a positive step. With the proper reinforcement and reward system, the newly acquired knowledge might just translate as hoped. If nothing else, it is one more issue that can be eliminated as a barrier to improved performance.

- Behavior change (in my personal opinion anyway) is what training is all about. It is not reasonable to put the full burden of business results on performance improvement interventions. Until the training, OD, and learning and development departments have significant control over business strategies and direction, they can only influence business results narrowly, not control them.

---

[8] As an author, I am constantly on my guard to avoid the use of trite, overworked, and hackneyed phrases. Sometimes the pressure just builds up and I have to get them out—thanks for understanding.

Those are some of the arguments in support of the continuing use of the Kirkpatrick Model. Admittedly, the model may not provide all the answers that an organization needs to guide it successfully into the future. Nevertheless, the model may provide some valuable information that can be used for planning purposes, if the assessments are designed, applied, and interpreted correctly.

Perhaps the best way to get the most out of the measurements that Dr. Kirkpatrick suggested is to quit thinking of the four levels as "levels" at all. If we consider each of these measurement areas as separate pictures of what is going on, we can apply them as needed to collect the type of information that serves our specific needs at the time. This is really the essence of the whole science of applied psychometrics: figuring out what we want to know and then setting out to collect that needed information.

Let's consider applying the four "areas" that Dr. Kirkpatrick isolated relative to a typical corporate training program. Who can benefit from a carefully designed instrument? What kind of information might be obtained? Who would have an interest in the information (i.e., who are the stakeholders in the report)?

Area (Level)	Type of information that can be collected	Beneficiaries	Possible Stakeholders
Reaction	Perceived skill of presenter	Trainers/Facilitators	Trainer Training Manager
Reaction	Predicted/declared behavior change/perceived knowledge gain	Participants (it helps them self-reinforce learning when they write down what they learned)	Participants Operational manager of participants All levels of leadership Training Manager
Reaction	Perceived relevance of course to current business needs	Course developers Training Manager Marketing staff* Sales * *If it is a "public" offering intended to generate interest in the host company's products or services	Course developers Operational manager of participants All levels of leadership Training Manager Sales* Marketing* Executive leadership of presenting/hosting company* *If it is a "public" offering intended to generate interest in the host company's products or services

Possible confounding factors:

- Degree of participants' qualifications to properly rate or evaluate the trainer, her/his knowledge, or the ultimate relevance of the materials to job performance
- Manner and timing of survey
  - Was there sufficient time to complete it?
  - Did the trainer influence responses?
  - Did the survey ask the right questions the right way?
- Was the rating system itself accurate and responsive in capturing the intended reaction information?

Area (Level)	Type of Information That Can Be Collected	Beneficiaries	Possible Stakeholders
Learning	Perceived skill of presenter in presenting new information so it is retained	Trainers/Facilitators	Trainer Training Manager
Learning	Information about estimated knowledge gained	Participants (again, it helps them self-reinforce learning when they answer questions)	Participants Operational Manager of Participants All levels of leadership Training Manager
Learning	"Pre-Post" comparison of test scores to identify where and to what extent improvement occurred	Course Developers & Training Manager (to demonstrate effectiveness of program) Participants (as a confidence builder) HR, Legal, Others (if providing compliance training to prove sufficiency of effort and to avoid liability)	Course Developers Training Manager Operational Manager of Participants HR, Legal, Others
Learning	Whether an individual achieved a required "passing" score for some type of certification or qualification	Participant See "Stakeholders" for other possible beneficiaries	Participant Operational Manager of Participants Marketing/Sales (if it adds credibility to the organization) Training Manager (if charged with achieving certain numbers of certified personnel)

Possible confounding factors:

- Were the respondents motivated to do well?
- Was the test any good?
  - Was it a valid test of the knowledge it was testing for? (Ever have a bad test—one that tested for dumb stuff not related to the intended learning?)
  - Was it administered fairly (including timing, scoring, limited distractions)?

Area (Level)	Type of information that can be collected	Beneficiaries	Possible Stakeholders
Behavior	Self-reported attitude or behavioral change through: • Survey • Interview	Participants (as a reinforcement exercise)	Training Department (as a measure of success of program) Co-workers (who would benefit/want to see a behavioral change) Leadership (that sees the behavioral change as a precursor of organizational benefit)
Behavior	Observer-reported behavioral change through: • Multi-rater survey • Performance review • "Ride-along" or other formal coaching or mentoring process report	Participants (reinforcement/development) Observer (through increased awareness of skills) .	Training Department (as a measure of success of program) Co-workers (who would benefit/want to see a behavioral change) Leadership (that sees the behavioral change as a precursor of organizational benefit)
Behavior	Customer/client feedback forms or interviews	Customers/clients (by becoming more sophisticated consumers) Organization (by gaining critical feedback for improvement/recognition purposes)	Training Department (as a measure of success of program) Leadership (that sees the behavioral change as a precursor of organizational

			benefit) Marketing/Sales (success stories/case studies to enhance offerings)

Possible confounding factors:

- Were the respondents comfortable in being honest?

- Were the raters prepared to judge the behaviors (e.g., were they *looking* for the behaviors before being asked if they saw them)?

- Did the raters have enough evidence to be able to make an accurate judgment?

Area (Level)	Type of Infor- mation That Can Be Collected	Beneficiaries	Possible Stakeholders
Results	This area is already well-documented in terms of accounting reports and reports of other Key Perform- ance Indicators (KPIs); additional KPIs may be created as needed to measure training outcomes	Varies, but is likely to the benefit of any supervisors or man- agers who oversee the operations that produce the meas- ured KPIs, possibly also the individual contributors who directly affected the outcomes	Anyone who benefits from performance improvements in one or more areas; for that reason, the or- ganization as a whole to one degree or an- other

Possible confounding factors:

- Were there other conditions that had a large influence on outcomes?
  - o Economic conditions
  - o Addition or reduction of staff
  - o New or reduced competition
  - o Change in leadership, supervision, or procedures
  - o Price changes
- Are there demonstrated cause-and-effect relationships between the behaviors created and the outcomes pro- duced, or is it just an assumption that there is a relationship that could be erroneous?[9]

---

[9] There are a number of associations that are either just coincidental or are the result of another outside influence that affects the relation- ship. Say what? Did you know, for example, that the number of drownings in the USA rises as consumption of ice cream rises? The reason is not that people drown in ice cream, of course — it is that during warmer weather, more people eat ice cream than in colder weather. By the same token, more people are swimming in warmer weather. That, dear reader, is why cause and effect is so tricky. Now go dry off and have a bowl of ice cream.

These tables should illustrate that each of the areas discussed by Dr. Kirkpatrick have relevance to some, and often many, members of an organization, and to those who are customers or clients of organizations. They should also illustrate that, although there is a "handshake" relationship between the areas, there is room for other influences that could enhance (or inhibit) a direct relationship between positive results in one area and positive results in another. When it comes to evaluation of training programs and their effects, any of the areas that Donald Kirkpatrick suggested are certainly worthy of consideration. There are probably more that you could think of as well. Take, for example, evaluating the environment where the learning takes place. Is the organization supporting the training by encouraging and reinforcing key concepts? Are there tools and systems available to take advantage of the new skills? Are there reward and recognition programs to encourage use of the new learning? The list can go on and on. The main point of this chapter is to expand your understanding of what the four areas of evaluation can support, as well as what they can't. Dr. Kirkpatrick presented some great ideas. It is up to us to build on the system to make it more valuable.

One final note: this chapter was relatively technical and you are now on the brink of starting a new chapter about training ROI. Before you become paralyzed with panic at the prospect that the book is going to get too serious, rest assured that training ROI is such a ludicrous idea that it does not have to be treated with the same reverence as the Four Levels . . . and it certainly won't be. So if you never spent the money to go to a seminar or attend a class in how to perform training ROI, you will be able to chuckle your way through. If you did attend such a program, compare the ROI of the cost of this book against the many hundreds of dollars it cost for the seminar and let me know which was the better value.

Chapter 4: *Let's Finally Retire Training ROI*

We have all heard them—those interesting contradictions in terms used as a speaking or writing technique to add richness to a concept. They are called "oxymorons" (or to be grammatically precise, "oxymora"). When they are crafted artfully, oxymora can add power to the written or spoken word. Phrases like "a deafening silence" or "parting is such sweet sorrow" can conjure up intense personal images among listeners and readers. Frankly, most of us think more of the purely comic usage of oxymora (e.g., "jumbo shrimp") or the satirical oxymora that often carry a not-so-subtle message (e.g., "healthy tan" or "corporate culture"). The perceptive reader knows where we are headed. Yes, it is time to add still another phrase to the list: "training ROI."

No matter how many books are written about how to perform training ROI, no matter how wealthy some people have become promoting the idea, no matter how much it is believed in, it has one major drawback: it doesn't work. Oh certainly, people can use any number of processes to research relevant data. They can interview participants, stakeholders, and managers about estimated benefits. They can use all manner of formulae, both simple and complex, to arrive at monetary values that can then be compared and contrasted to other expenses or even actual investments. The

> No matter how many books are written about . . . ROI . . . it has one major drawback: **it doesn't work**.

bottom-line problem is that training ROI must depend on the same thing that makes a good fiction novel: there must be suspension of disbelief.

In order to be able to enjoy H.G. Wells's novel, *The Time Machine* at its most fundamental level, one has to be willing to accept that it is possible for someone at the end of the nineteenth-century to be able to build such a device in his home study. To enjoy Superman comics or movies as we did as children, we have to accept the premise that, of course someone coming to earth from the planet Krypton would have super powers.

By the same token, in order to accept the idea that we can actually compute the Return on Investment training program, we have to accept the following "facts":

- We can take an expense and think of it as an investment.

(Please write me as soon as you hear of someone who bought a training program from a vendor then later sold it back to the vendor [or anyone else] for a profit—then it will have become an *investment*—until then, it is an expense, just like the lunch you enjoyed yesterday.)

- Training drives business "results."

(Any and all training directors who have the authority to marshal and direct their marketing, production, legal, and sales divisions in support of their training, please write me as well—if you don't have oversight of those areas, you aren't "driving" business results—you may *support* business initiatives but you can't *control* them in any significant way.)

- We can actually get everyone in an organization to take our ROI calculations seriously.

(Virtually all organizations, for-profit, not-for-profit, or governmental have people who were trained and work in a "world" of business principles and accounting procedures. Those folks are going to have a hard time agreeing that someone has accurately captured the true cost ["investment" if you prefer] of any training program. Those same folks are going to have a hard time with any precise measure of the "return," probably challenging the figures by suggesting that other departments like R&D, production, and sales contributed handsomely to the bottom line in greater percentages than the training ROI report suggests. Other people may also chime in with the bean counters in questioning how anyone could put a dollar value on "motivation," "good will," or "customer loyalty," which all plays a role in the final business results.)

- There is some point to doing the calculations anyway.

(This is the real challenge—let's say that those who were performing a training ROI were completely unbiased, and let's say those using the results were initially willing to do away with any and all training programs that did not generate a sufficient ROI. Is any organization going to eliminate popular programs for employees just because the dollar return was not sufficient relative to other programs? Before assuming they might, consider this extrapolation: If ROI was the sole governing consideration, every business would likely be considering elimination of every department, program, and expense that did not produce profits directly, including employee benefits, disaster insurance, accounting departments, and security. Consider movie theaters—they make their profit from selling $6 bags of popcorn and $5 cups of cola—to turn a profit really, they could eliminate the movies and just invite people in to the theater to buy food—an ill-advised idea.)

The astute reader has by now arrived at the conclusion that there are some significant flaws in the whole training ROI concept. This would probably be a partial explanation for why less than 5 percent of training departments ever even attempt to conduct them.[10]

Just to conclude the chapter at this point would not really be fair; after all, the concept of being able to put a value on training using the language of business and accounting might be of value in some organizations. The good news is there are objective, quantifiable measures that can be used, but it is also important to realize that no matter how many objective measures we come up with, it will not tell the full story of what the training function has done. Let's consider just one more illustration and then no more fooling around. The next several chapters take a hard look at measures that count, so to speak.[11]

The Problem with Completely Objective Measures

Okay. You have just visited the Louvre in Paris where you had an opportunity to view the Mona Lisa. A beloved

---

[10] J. Bersin, *High-Impact Learning Measurement: Best Practices, Models, and Business-Driven Solutions for the Measurement and Evaluation of Corporate Training* 2006, (Bersin & Associates: 11 November: 2006), PDF.

[11] For those who absolutely positively have to have objective measures of training outcomes and who are willing to live with the built-in weaknesses, there are a few very simple measurement examples presented in Appendix A.

great aunt of yours wants to hear all about the Mona Lisa. She is known by you to be a lover of fine art, but has never really had the means to travel to Paris to view it firsthand.

"Ah-h-h," you exclaim, "The Mona Lisa. Well, Aunt Grace, what can I tell you? Let me see . . ." As you reflect, you can see the anticipation in her still-clear, bright eyes. The words come to you.

"In a nutshell, it is a 30 X 21 inch oil painting on a poplar panel. I noticed that there is a fine crack in the paint, which extends from the top of the panel just about down to her hairline, probably from poor storage years ago. It is of course now in a temperature controlled, bullet-proof case today—but you want to know about the painting! Silly me!"

The smile has faded somewhat from your aunt's lips. You continue.

"It is probably a really good likeness of this woman, but how would I know? She probably died over 350 years ago (chuckle). What I mean is that it looked like somebody probably would've looked like back then. Anyway, it is a half-length portrait so I couldn't see her feet, but if I looked carefully, the eyes kind of followed me—I think. I'm not sure if everybody notices that, but I did."

If you concentrate, you can visualize your sweet, dear aunt hauling off and clobbering you with her cane. Why? Because your description was largely made up of objective, quantitative elements of the experience without benefit of any personal, subjective reaction. In so doing, the essence of what makes the Mona Lisa arguably the most famous painting in history is lost.

Measuring What Counts

Okay, the idea of performing or selling training ROI is pointless. But for those of you who want to have a way of quantifying training outcomes, we still need to offer a solution. At some level most of us do want training outcome quantification. It is only natural that if we are working hard to affect the bottom line of a business operation, it would be good to have some type of way of quantifying both the effort and the results. What follows are some hints about ways we can do just that without relying on the wrong tools.

Our first challenge is to identify the effect[s] we need to measure that are at least somewhat within our control. Just like marketing, accounting, IT, and other support departments, training does not have a way of *directly* affecting most of the standard business measures. Nevertheless, all the support departments are valuable because they do *influence* the business measures, albeit somewhat indirectly. In other words, training someone in proper sales techniques does not directly increase sales volume, but if the learned skills are properly employed, sales volume will likely increase. The catch is that the effort (sales training) is removed from the business effect (sales volume) by at least one degree. Therefore, we should strive to obtain a reasonable measure of training effects that can effectively serve as leading indicators of business results. If there is a strong, clear correlation, that is almost as good as a direct relationship.

Measures of Success

In summary, to assess the value of training, we need to remember the key elements that all combine to produce the data we can in turn use as a leading indicator:

- Training is intended to alter behaviors; the altered behaviors in turn affect outcomes.
- In that training is affecting behavior change (not business results directly), we should be measuring *only* behavior changes, instead of chasing after equivocal business results.
- If we can manage to *reinforce* the behavior changes through the *process* of measuring them, so much the better.
- Behavior change is not measured with a snap-shot—it is measured with time-lapse photography.

Those points and more will be covered in the following chapters. Isn't it amazing how much interesting and useful information a small book like this can hold?

Chapter 5: *Exploiting the Uncertainty Principle: You Will Affect the Outcome*

Some Important Principles

About eighty years ago, a physicist by the name of Werner Heisenberg established a principle that directly applies to measurement of training outcomes. His "Uncertainty Principle" basically said that the simple act of measuring something *alters* the properties of whatever is measured.[12] In other words, when we measure training outcomes or behavior changes, we affect those outcomes. This fact can be used to our advantage. If we think about it, we are really more interested in *improving* performance than just reporting measures of it. As discussed in earlier chapters, there is much effort and time spent on making assessments more precise. It seems, though, that little thought has ever been given to harnessing the behavioral change effects of observation and measurement. Considering the effort required to perform assessments of performance, wouldn't you rather think that assessments were performing the secondary task of reinforcing desired changes, even if some precision was lost, rather than thinking that the measurements were "spot on" accurate but doing nothing to make things better?

---

[12] For the absolute purists among us, it is acknowledged that the Uncertainty Principle is misquoted and misused here. Nevertheless, this interpretation was popularized in the film *Jurassic Park* and who are we to challenge popular dogma? A more appropriate theorem might be what is known among behaviorists as the "Observer Effect." Regardless of what theory supports the ideas here, they are terrific concepts so don't worry about whose ideas I stole — they work.

The points discussed below boil down to this:
- Let them know how the assessment will be of personal benefit.
- Let them know it will be fair and balanced, so they can trust it.
- Keep it confidential — don't throw a huge spotlight on the people being rated.
- Be sure the people making the ratings can be trusted to do a good job.
- Don't let anybody get in trouble for being honest.
- Use it to make things better — don't use it as an excuse to punish.

Performance improvement does not automatically come about as a result of taking measures and making assessments. The measurement/assessment strategy must be designed and implemented in a way that produces improvement. This can be done with relative ease as long as certain guiding principles are employed. The principles are listed below:
- Subjects being measured must know that the measurements will only be used to benefit them personally; there can be no direct downside cost to the results produced.
- The subjects must have a conscious way to link the measurements being taken to factors they can influence or control; they have to feel that they can positively affect the outcomes.

- The system of measurement should include a means by which the subjects can rate, evaluate, or discuss factors that affect their performance but that are not within their control (external performance factors).
- To the greatest extent possible, given the purpose of the assessment, knowledge of individual performance ratings should be restricted to the individual being rated and and to those others with a need to know only; adults react adversely to being judged, rated, classified, etc. etc. unless the assessment is part of a program supporting their own voluntary self-improvement.

> No one goes on vacation with plans to take only a single photo.
>
> No one goes on a diet and steps on the scale just one time.
>
> Why would we choose to measure the behavioral changes from a major training initiative just once?

- Those who are charged with performing a measurement or rating of other people need to be adequately prepared for the task, along with being provided with enough opportunity to do a competent job; don't ask people to rate things about which they are unfamiliar, disinterested, or unprepared.
- Those who rate or measure organizational superiors need to be assured that they will not be penalized in any way for making an honest evaluation — this is generally done by

- Protecting the anonymity of peer and subordinate raters.
- Those who rate organizational subordinates need to be trained and prepared to deal positively with challenges presented by those they rate, as well as being prepared to objectively support their ratings non-defensively.
- The data being provided should be significantly more informational (i.e., used for planning and development purposes) than evaluative (i.e., used to rank or classify past behaviors for the purpose of further judgment or reward/penalty).

Capturing Actionable Information

Many of us take cameras and video recorders with us on vacation so we can share our experiences with others or at least personally reminisce. It would be absurd to plan to go on vacation with the intention of taking just one photo, or capturing a five-second video segment of the trip to represent the entire experience. By the same token, it does not make much sense to take a single measurement "snapshot" of on-going behavioral change in order to draw conclusions based on that single data point, either.

To further clarify, consider this analogy: You decide to go on a diet to lose fifteen pounds. Would it be likely that you would choose just one or two times to weigh yourself and then stop? Of course not! If you are watching your eating habits (a behavioral change) you want to know frequently how you are doing. No one is going to just weigh himself one time and on that basis, decide whether a diet is working and when it is complete. You need and want ongoing information to know not only if it is working, but how well and how long it needs to continue. By the same token, considering our previously listed guiding principle, to make data informational rather than evaluative, there is a real need for more data than we can get from just one sampling.

How much data gathering is enough? Strictly speaking, it all depends on two factors: how fast can behavioral change be expected to happen, and how much tolerance does your audience have for measurement?

In a "measurement perfect" world, I suppose we would slap some magical electrodes on a subject and continuously monitor behaviors, tracking outcomes like an earthquake seismograph. Aside from the impracticality, human nature is not such that continuous monitoring (using electrodes or anything else for that matter) would be tolerated. For many organizations, conducting even occasional assessments results in an outcry of "survey fatigue!" and "we're getting measured to death." This creates a challenge for sure, but not an insurmountable one. This issue will be addressed presently.

For now, let's switch our focus to the easier of the two factors—the question of "how quickly can behavioral changes be observed and measured/assessed?"

The short answer is that we can start recording *anticipated* changes right away. The observable ones take a little longer, but that does not mean that we cannot gather actionable information almost immediately. When we consider how any behavioral change happens, we realize that we have to look no further than inside our own minds. For fun, start doing *anything* without thinking of it first. Get up and get a drink of water. Cross and uncross your legs. Look out the window. Any action (behavior) that you undertake, whether new and untested or familiar, is preceded by thought. There was, if only for a fleeting moment, a conceptualization of the action and a decision to take the action. For activities that are extremely familiar to us, this process "feels" unconscious and automatic. It isn't automatic. Be glad of that; otherwise, who knows what sorts of things we would be doing automatically, without thought or consideration of consequence? It would be like living in a world entirely populated by adolescents—a chilling vision for sure.

Activities and behaviors that are new or different seldom happen so effortlessly. Think about the first time you operated a motor vehicle or rode a bicycle. Every action was consciously deliberated, every move performed tentatively. As time went on and the functions became more familiar, it was easy to recognize how much improvement was happening. If you were asked if you were any better at staying balanced on your first "two-wheeler," it would be very easy for you to answer; after all, who knows better how you are performing a skill than you yourself?

Let's go back even earlier in the behavior change cycle than practiced activity. We'll go back to the point of "original intention." Let's consider that diet to lose fifteen pounds. You have managed to muster up the motivation, you have read the books, and you have gone on the internet and found great-sounding diet recipes. Perhaps you even worked out an exercise program that you could live with. Right before you start your weight loss efforts, if

you were surveyed and asked what changes you anticipated, what challenges you thought you might encounter,
and what success you would have by a certain date, you
would have some kind of answer. It might not prove to be
totally accurate, but there is a good chance that you
would be close in your estimates, at least in the short
term.

Moreover, what if you publicly declared what those
fitness goals and anticipated outcomes would be?
Wouldn't such a declaration provide you with at least a
little more motivation to prove yourself correct and avoid
having to acknowledge failure?
Think back now to the Heisenberg Uncertainty Principle.
Simply declaring to another person (even through a survey)
what your diet and exercise program was going to do most likely
affected your motivation and
clarified your vision of success.
That is part of how measurements and assessments can help
to further the desired goal.

> Who knows what
> sorts of things we
> would be doing
> automatically,
> without thought or
> consideration of
> consequence? It
> would be like liv-
> ing in a world
> entirely populated
> by adolescents—a
> chilling vision for
> sure.

So for now, we have established that some feedback can be
provided almost immediately following a training (behavioral) intervention. Now it is time to return to the issue of
how much can we assess without driving our subjects to
distraction and without spending inordinate amounts of
time engaged in measurement activities. Every organization will have its own "tolerance." For most, it is probably

fair to assume that people would be willing to supply feedback every forty-five days or so if the assessments were properly linked to an ongoing training initiative. This time estimate is only approximate. It is reasonable to increase or decrease the time span by about a third without any noticeable effect in outcomes. The trick is in knowing how to go about it.

It is important to remember that from the subject employee's perspective, the only "good" reason for taking measurements or performing assessments about her/his behavior is for the purpose of professional or personal self-development. If employees feel that they are being monitored and evaluated for purposes of punishment (or even reward), the emotional fatigue will become uncomfortable for them. The average adult wants to feel a sense of control over her/his behaviors and activities; therefore, the assessments need to reinforce that feeling, not undermine it.

If we consider our first suggested assessment, the "anticipatory" or predictive assessment, the only person qualified to estimate what changes will happen with any degree of certainty is the individual subject personally. No one else knows what he or she sees as potential results or barriers as clearly as the person starting to make the changes. This data can inform an organization of several things:

- level of motivation of the subject
- areas where support would be welcomed
- what the initial outcomes are anticipated to be (for planning purposes)

The payoff for this initial assessment also includes the effect of reinforcing the learning/behavioral objectives of the initiative in a way that is not at all intimidating and is in fact empowering for the subject. This is actually an opportunity for the person to evaluate the training experience and to call for needed support to help ensure the success of the overall effort. In a nutshell, everyone wins by having this assessment at this time.

The second assessment, delivered about forty-five days post-training, works in similar fashion. Again, the individual alone is being asked to respond. There is still no outside evaluation being done at all. In short, the subject simply indicates the degree to which anticipated improvements (changes) are occurring. This approach is analogous to feedback about our diet program. We have been watching what we eat, have been exercising, and are making some progress. Maybe we are enjoying a feeling of improved well-being and the scale is showing a 6–8 pound weight loss. All the signs are indicating that the program is working well. To go out and ask an impartial (translated "uninvolved") third party how well the fitness program is working would not likely get the depth or accuracy of information needed. After all, when was the last time you really noticed that someone had lost seven pounds? That which is barely perceptible to an outside observer might be profoundly recognized by the individual.

When it comes to business/professional behavioral changes, the same reasoning applies. An employee could be enjoying significant personal success in improving her or his listening skills, time management skills, probing skills, or a variety of other behaviors that will ultimately reflect very well on his/her performance personally as well as on the organization. But let's be real.

As outsiders who already have a perception about the individual, can we say that we will notice these gradual changes so soon? Not likely—we are, after all, deeply engaged in worrying about ourselves most of the time. It's hard enough for some of us to remember to pick up the dry cleaning and to feed the dog. Are we really going to notice if a work associate is more "actively" listening to a conversation?

Let's review where we are and where we are going. Up to this point, we have attempted to alter behaviors and asked early on if the message was well received and what we could expect. About a month and a half later, we asked for more direct feedback to validate the initial predictions. This has, up to this point, been somewhat of a personal expression of commitment on the part of the subject without any outside parties making judgments about the outcomes. In business, though, a simple pronouncement of "I'm doing great" is not a solid enough foundation to justify continuation of a training program. After all, what if the subject is just wanting to look good or is simply going along to get along?

The time has arrived to validate the supposed outcomes. This means that someone besides the subject has to take notice and somehow evaluate what the investment has wrought in terms of business benefit. There is a procedure that must be followed to get good information from these "objective" sources, however. Remember, most of us are largely consumed by things important to us. After all, it really is all about us anyway, so how much effort can we really spend worrying about others?

All of us know that the claim that "it is really all about

us" isn't entirely true. Maybe in a perfect world it would be, but occasionally, we must divert our attention away from our own immediate self-interest. That being the case, we may as well do it right.

Okay, we are supposed to rate Amber and Troy on how well they are facilitating team meetings since taking that class on team building. What are we supposed to do? It's hard to remember what Amber did at the last meeting, and I know Troy said things went well, but was that before or after the training session?

This is likely pretty much what we go through when asked to evaluate someone else on some sliver of performance outcomes. It is not easy to recall with any certainty who did what when, unless it was something really notable. But by the same token, it is not in our nature to respond to questions with a series of "I don't know," "Not observed," "Can't recall" answers. After all, we are being counted on to give feedback. Okay, let's think of something we can react to . . . nothing. Nada. We really can't even much remember if we were at the last couple of meetings! Well, one thing is

> If we could somehow go back and look at the averages of all the ratings for everything that used a 1–5 scale of performance . . . the average would be somewhere between 3.8 and 4.2.

fairly safe—we can say that both Amber and Troy are doing "slightly better than average." In most cases, that is what? A "4" on a 1–5 scale? That should work. And if we can remember anything specific, we can throw in a couple of "3" and "5" scores for color. That's the ticket!

Sound familiar? It should. If we could somehow go back and look at the averages of all the ratings for everything that used a 1–5 scale of performance across all organizations since Rensis Likert developed his iconic "Likert Scaling System" in the 1940s, I am here to bet that the average would be somewhere between 3.8 and 4.2.

This is based on a few principles. First, those of us who grew up in the United States sometime during the twentieth-century had it ingrained that "if you can't say something nice, don't say anything at all." So who are we to shrug off years of parental-figure indoctrination and enforcement? Second, how would we like it if somebody who didn't know how we performed some activity rated *us* lower than "above average?" (We also learned our "Golden Rule" at about the same time.) Third, what kind of rater would we look like if we didn't have some kind of an opinion? People might start wondering what we did all day.

The list of motivators can go on and on, but this is a good start. The question then becomes, "If this is the result we can expect in most cases, what can we do about it?" Fortunately, there is a process. Remember the survey that went out at the forty-five-day point? There is another element to that survey. We let the subject know that with the *next* assessment, we are going to be *validating* the changes with some other folks who the subject works with. Not right then, but in about a month and a half. There are no secrets about this process.

The subjects are told at the time of the forty-five-day survey (or very shortly after) exactly who will be asked to rate them. The subjects are informed that the raters will be provided with exactly the same items that the subjects are responding to in the current survey. About the same time, the raters are also informed that they will be encouraged to look at the list of behavioral items to be assessed and given the names of the subjects they will be rating. Lastly, both groups (subjects and raters) will be encouraged to discuss the upcoming multi-rater process and how they can best observe and be observed. This way, they have roughly forty-five days to stay tuned into each other so that honest, balanced ratings can be made. A common side effect (benefit) is that with all the attention being placed on the upcoming ninety-day assessment, the behaviors will be more effectively practiced. There we go with that Uncertainty Principle again. We are using the simple act of assessment preparation to enhance the performance of the behaviors. Then as promised, at about the ninety-day mark, the sub-

> **Behavioral Measurement Success in Three Phases**
>
> Day 1–5: Predictive (anticipatory) Assessment
>
> Day 40–50 Verification Self Assessment
>
> Day 80–100 Multi-Rater Validation Study

jects are asked to verify their own behavioral changes once again while the raters are asked to rate and comment on what they saw (to validate the changes). No surprises and limited anxiety for anyone—the end result is feedback from two perspectives about what has been going on in terms of behavioral change. The most important outcome is the likely improvement gain resulting from the active assessment process. Dr. Heisenberg, we salute both you and your Uncertainty Principle!

Chapter 6: *The Only Information That Matters Is Actionable Information*

Warren Buffet, the philanthropist, billionaire, former U.S. Representative, author, and all-around smart business guy is also known for his pithy quotes about business. Two of those quotes seem particularly appropriate to kick off this chapter: "If past history was all there was to the game, the richest people would be librarians" and, "In the business world, the rearview mirror is always clearer than the windshield." Mr. Buffet captured part of the essence of what successful business operations do on a consistent daily basis to remain competitive: they look at the next anticipated change in circumstances so they can be ready for the environmental changes when they arrive. Historical reports are fine for the Monday-morning quarterbacks and analysts but they do limited duty when it comes to guiding future direction.

Of course, it is important to learn from past experience to avoid repeating mistakes. The problem with reliance on past performance to predict future outcomes is that past performance is not necessarily going to tell you all you need to know when circumstances change. For example, do this: Tell a friend or associate a really funny joke, and deliver it with perfect comedic timing that gets him laughing so hard that his eyes tear up and his sides hurt. Now, as soon as your friend catches his breath, go ahead and tell him the exact same joke again exactly the same way. See any drawbacks? The same principle applies to business and training. Just because an initiative or program went well one time does not mean that it will have the same outcome when reapplied. To assume that one outcome predicts another is courting problems.[13] It is important to design initiatives with an eye to anticipated outcomes. We all know that. No legitimate ad campaign is ever created without extensive discussion and speculation as to what effects it will have. No major business realignment is ever undertaken without careful consideration of what the risks and benefits may be.

By the same token, down the road following implementation, there is plenty of conversation as to how things turned out. There is a missing element, however. That element consists of influencing or enhancing the outcome from the point of launch and before the postmortem reports start rolling in.

It's time for another analogy. Assume you are a surgeon performing a delicate heart surgery on an elderly woman. What are the odds that you would plan the procedure, discuss it with the patient and staff, do the surgery, and then just wish for the best for the next year until you hear back from the patient as to how she is feeling? In all probability, you would be vitally concerned during the process about what the various monitors were telling you, along with regular feedback from the anesthetist, surgical nurse, assisting physicians, and your own observations. And why, you ask? Because the success of the operation is critically dependent on what is going on during the procedure. And why, you ask? Because you can control factors affecting the outcome more directly at

---

[13] For those of you who are behavioral event interview (BEI) fans, please understand that although past behavior correlates well with future behavior it does not correlate significantly with performance outcomes — performance (just like in the joke example) is influenced by a myriad of other contextual factors

that time than at any other point. And why, you ask? Because during that time, you are in the best position to do things differently if you need to than at any other time. This same approach applies equally well to:

- Automobile trips
- Child rearing
- House construction
- Dieting
- Knife fights
- Closing the barn door before all the horses have gone
- Training initiatives

All this leads us to yet another important measurement principle.

Generally Unacknowledged Measurement Principle #5:
If you want measurement to influence the outcome of the process you are measuring positively, you need to measure outcomes during the event process. Only current and timely measurements provide completely actionable information.

Operations Live and Die by Actionable Information
Up to this point, the term "actionable information" has been used without definition as a cheap literary ploy to keep you reading to find out what it means. Your persistence has paid off. Actionable information is at least partial evidence and data that you can use to influence future critical outcomes. It is the highest and best use of assessment and measurement data and has

been used for years in manufacturing with direct application to people.

The concept of Statistical Process Control was developed back in the 1920s to reduce waste and to improve production efficiencies, by Walter A. Shewhart, and later employed by W. Edwards Deming to improve the quality of munitions production during World War II (here we go with that bomb stuff again . . .). In short, it was based on basic mathematical statistics theories to identify when mass production operations were performing well and when adjustments were needed to be made to avoid producing products that would not meet standards. If, during a manufacturing cycle, it was discovered that products were being turned out that were outside of tolerance limits, the manufacturing line would be shut down so that adjustments could be made to bring everything back into line well before the QC (quality control) folks would have to intervene and throw out valuable materials.

The same principle applies to the use of measurement data during and immediately following a training initiative. Rather than waiting weeks or months perhaps to discover that the training did not get the results desired, it is possible to identify areas where adjustments can be made almost immediately to get the desired behavioral outcomes. That is the essence of actionable information: getting information in time to be able to use it as the process moves forward to enhance and control for the effects of an initiative.

Then there is the psychological perspective. If you think about it, many (not all but many) executives share a common trait: they like to fix problems. If you have had the experience of working with a classic executive leader, you can probably relate to the idea that they are happiest when they are controlling resources and commanding action to get results. Tell an executive that everything is going well and she will probably find something wrong with your analysis or at least seem slightly agitated. Tell her that you are having a problem with something, and you will see her immediately spring into command and control mode to resolve whatever is not working well. What she probably won't say is that she is delighted that she has a problem to fix—it is her raison d'être—her essential purpose, her reason to exist. By supplying such leaders with ongoing information about the successes and challenges associated with your latest intervention, you not only keep the boss engaged, you find that you may have a powerful ally supporting and driving the outcomes you promised in the first place.

> For business outcomes to change, the way business is conducted has to change.

It's All About Behavioral Change Anyway

Before we bid *adieu* to this chapter, we should come back around to some fundamentals as they apply to training and other organizational interventions and initiatives. We need to remember that training events, policy changes, and organizational paradigm shifts are intended primarily to do one thing[14]:

---

[14] There are actually two or more hoped for outcomes if you consider the personal desires of champions of an initiative—they have their own personal agendas of fame, fortune, or power within the organization. In this book we pretend that people are selflessly motivated

Affect business outcomes in a desired direction. For business outcomes to change, the way business is conducted has to change. In most cases, this calls for behavioral change on the part of the organizational members. That is why behavioral change is considered a leading indicator of business change and the reason that organizations want to measure it. Organizations do not typically institute training interventions to amuse those involved, or to add to the existing body of knowledge. Of course, both of those outcomes may occur, but those effects are not why the programs are being initiated. Neither one of them correlates very well with behavioral change anyway.

Given those fundamentals, it is wise for those of us involved with the implementation of interventions (training or other) to remember that somebody wants to see behaviors change. Those same "some bodies" think they know what the behavioral change is that they want to see. The sooner they can see that change, the better they like it (and you). If the change is not what they want, the sooner they can alter the outcomes, the better they like it (and you). Word to the wise: Let the "some bodies" know early and often what changes they are getting and they will really like that (and you). You deserve to be liked, right?

---

team players rather than the dogs they really are. My next book deals with that.

Chapter 7: *Engage Your Respondents: They Will Spill Their Guts Out*

U p to this point, the emphasis has been placed on some of the more technical aspects of measurement and assessment—the structure, timing, data collection methods, and design. All of that is important, but even the best planned, designed, and administered assessment strategy will fall short of its intended mark if we forget the sources of our information: the people we are polling. After all, a survey or assessment is kind of like asking a stranger for a favor: "Excuse me, but would you mind taking several minutes out of your day so I can collect what may feel like really personal information about you so I can tell somebody else what you said?" Although there are a few people who might respond positively to a request like that, it is probably safe to assume that the majority would not. ("Say what?!? Do I know you or something?")

Such has been the burden of the pollster since early caveman days (I assume). People are not particularly inclined to give of themselves in such large measures if there is no apparent benefit that will be afforded to them. They, reasonably enough, have other more pressing issues that they could spend  their time on, like walking their pet iguana, or buying lottery tickets, just to name a couple. The good news is that there is one fairly widespread human characteristic that can be exploited very effectively if properly positioned.

Generally Unacknowledged Measurement Principle #6:
Most people feel they have better things to do than to answer questions. However, most people also think they are smarter than you. If asked properly, they will tell you all about themselves and their world in hopes of impressing you with their insight and wisdom.

There you have it. Surveys will get fairly open and honest responses if the respondents think there is even a tiny chance that their thoughts and opinions will somehow be listened to and valued. So how does one go about creating that atmosphere? So glad you wondered—that is what the rest of this chapter is all about.

Making Your Survey Engaging
There are a few things that you can do to enhance the likelihood that you will get the type of responses you are hoping for from your survey or assessment.

- Even if completion of the assessment is somehow "required" or "expected" (as part or one's job for example) make it feel voluntary to the respondent—be humble as if they are doing you a favor.
- Lavish praise on the respondents for even considering responding.
- Tell the respondents how their answers and reactions are going to influence something.
- Although you are using the written word, ask questions in such a way that it feels as if you are having a casual conversation with them—

including using slang and conversational grammar.

- Keep the number of question items as small as you can—nobody likes feeling like they are being interrogated.
- Keep the tone of the questions light, positive, and even "fun" to the greatest extent possible.
- Ask mostly about personal feelings as opposed to judgments—it is easier to react with less "test fatigue" than would be present in more conventional surveys, regardless of length.

Let's look at each point in greater detail.

Make Them Feel Like They Are Doing You a Favor

Frankly, they *are* doing you a favor; ever hear the old expression, "You can lead a horse to water, but you can't make him drink"? Well, you can't get him to carefully fill out a survey, either. The same reasoning applies to people in regards to both drinking and survey taking. Horses and people are *motivated* more easily than they are *coerced*, and when it comes to survey respondents, the best motivators are (1) creating guilt feelings for not completing the survey, (2) enticements, or (3) providing some self-satisfaction derived from completion of the process. I have a tendency to work on the self-satisfaction angle, myself.

Tactics like including a dollar with a "thank you" for completing the survey the bill is attached to seem kind of heavy-handed. It is obvious that the money is intended to create a sense of obligation (the antecedent of guilt for the procrastinators among us). Guilt is generally not a good footing upon which to collect balanced feedback. People are already a bit edgy before they even start the process.

Enticements such as, "You will (upon completion) be automatically entered into a drawing for a dinner for two at the beautiful *Coûteux Nourriture* restaurant — just imagine!" have a tendency to switch attention from a careful response to questions to more basic drivers, like qualifying for the drawing. It's kind of like encouraging voters to get out and vote, early AND often.

Yes, I am a big fan of making the process the attraction itself. The first step is to be sure that the survey is relevant to the person getting it. People are happy to comment on things that affect them directly but could care less if they are not affected by the results. Next is to acknowledge that you need to have the survey completed, and that the respondent can be a big help. People like to feel important, especially if they are dealing with an issue that is important to them. The added touch of telling the respondent how the responses will be used is a real good motivator and helps them to stay involved — they better realize that their opinions/reactions matter. Then if you make the survey somehow engaging so that it has at least a little entertainment value — wow, you have a winner.

Lavishing Praise (Kissing Up)

Did I mention how kind it was of you to buy this book? And now you are reading it — it just doesn't get any better! Okay, I was kissing up just a bit right there but it made you smile, right? Of course it did, and the same thing will happen when you toss a little praise and gratitude at your respondents. We all can use a little more gratitude for our efforts and when we get it, there is a tendency to respond positively, which is what this is all about—responding. Did you know that "response rate" is one of the primary tools to determine if a survey is any good? It makes sense when you think about it. The more of your target group you have giving you feedback, the greater the likelihood that you have usable, actionable information (assuming the respondents paid attention to their answers). As we all know, you attract more flies with honey than you do with vinegar. (I am just a bit unclear as to why anyone would want to attract flies in the first place, but that is neither here nor there. Let's proceed.)

Let Them Know They Are Affecting Things

Ever give much thought to changing the world? For those of you who can call yourselves "baby boomers" (born between about 1946 and 1963), the collective desire for world change is a commonly assigned attribute of your generational cohort. I don't know why it got associated with boomers, though. Anyone above the age of nineteen has, at least for a short while, expressed a desire to make the world different. I personally think that we all kind of keep that fantasy alive in some part of our psyche, just waiting for opportunities to bring it out, dust it off, and set about changing things. That is part of what makes well-designed surveys so . . . so . . . well designed. A good survey lets the respondents know that what they say is going to be looked at and taken into consideration to make the object of the survey somehow better.

On a side note, that is why so many "smiley sheets" at the end of a corporate training class or those end-of-

"As soon as you fill out the class evaluation form, you can leave."

course surveys that you got in college are such a joke. The same forms are sent out over and over again, asking the same things of essentially the same people, with absolutely no change in anything resulting from all that effort. It is no wonder that people will do just about anything to get the forms filled out and escape the classroom. I once saw a student **literally chew his own leg off in order to escape the classroom** to avoid filling out the same survey he had responded to ten times before.[15]

Getting back on track, the essential elements to address this motivation are:

- Explain that the survey is for the express purpose of creating change based on feedback.
- Only ask about those things for which you are ready, willing, and able to make changes (i.e., if you cannot change the location of the classroom,

---

[15] That is, of course, a bold-faced lie; I never saw such a thing. But, in that you are reading this footnote, you might find it interesting to note that my bold-faced lie actually was a **boldface** lie, meaning the lie was printed in *bold face type*, which is where the expression came from way back in 1591. "Barefaced lie" was actually in print in 1590. The common idiom error of "bald face lie" was not seen before 1943. This is all courtesy of the kind folks at Merriam Webster (really). Is this not the most fascinating footnote you ever read?

don't ask if it was a good place to have class; if there are 1,000 participant guides already printed that *will* be used, don't ask if they should be changed).

- Actually use and report back to the respondents what you find out and what you intend to do with the information.

If those three elements are consistently delivered, not only will the response rate and quality be better than average, it will tend to improve over time.

Hold a Survey "Conversation" With Your Respondents

Surveys have traditionally not held a great deal of interest for most people. Consider the following activities:

- Watching a *Leave it to Beaver* re-run marathon on a warm, sunny day while on your Hawaiian vacation
- Finally sorting all the loose screws and nails into their proper containers that have been sitting on the bottom of your old toolbox
- Counting how many semi-trailer trucks you see on the highway between El Paso and Oklahoma City during a family-driving vacation
- Attending traffic violation school
- Completing a survey

If we are ever to get "completing a survey" off of the list, we have to do something to engage the respondent. This is most easily accomplished by using the written word to "talk" to them rather than to "survey" them. Consider the following examples:

Traditional	Way Better
Rate the instructor	How good a job did the instructor do from *your* perspective?
Rate the materials	Were the handouts better than average? Why? (With options to check including an "other" choice.)
Rate the course	Thinking about other courses you have had, was this one more interesting (or helpful or informative), less interesting, or about the same?
Rate the service you received on this visit	Did the service you got exceed your expectations? Please tell us why so we can get better.
Please check the box that approximates your wait time before being helped	Considering everything, was your experience worth the wait? If not, what should we do about it?

The biggest difference is that the questions are written the way you might ask them if you were talking to the respondent. There is something about that approach that keeps people engaged and honest about their responses. The traditional format looks and reads like the most boring scientific study ever devised. The "Way Better" format involves and challenges the respondent to state ideas and opinions. In summary, it is the difference between reading this book on measurement and assessment and just about any other book on the topic. The other books stink. This one is terrific. Am I right? I rest my case.

Keep It Short—or as Short as Possible, Anyway

We need never to lose sight of the fact that sentient beings are complex. Notice that I did not say "human" beings—I said "sentient" beings. This includes dogs, cats, porcupines, iguanas, and Koala bears—just about any creature that reacts on the basis of multiple sensory stimuli. That is then just about any creature with a beating heart (except for the dope you got stuck behind on the freeway yesterday). The complexity comes from the process of receiving multiple stimuli (sometimes hundreds or thousands of stimuli in the course of even a minute) and processing it all to end up with an ever-changing set of feelings and reactions at any given time. Interestingly enough, even though the reactions we have might be in a constant state of flux, somewhere in our brains we can retain the memory of the totality of feeling that we had in the minutes, days, months, or even years of the past if the feelings were strong enough. Details might fade, but most of us can pretty clearly summon up the emotions associated with past experiences.

Take a moment to think back to events major and minor in your life—think back to personally significant childhood and adolescent events (like your first kiss, a visit to Grandma's house, playing with your favorite puppy, kitten, or weasel, etc.). Details may have become fuzzy, but you can recall the sensations, right? Okay, now hold that thought while we go on for a minute.

What does all this have to do with surveys? In a word, *everything*. Let's take the example of a training program that you attended as part of your personal or professional development. The more recent, the better, but any one will do. For most of us, we have certain overall feelings about the experience, the instructor, the others in the class, what we learned, how we felt while we were there, and whether we got anything of value from it. The critical point to note here is that all those feelings were not produced in isolation. Take, for example, your impression of the instructor. Her or his eye contact with you and others might have played a role in your engagement at the time, as did the tone and volume of the instructor's voice, his/her body language, and overall appearance. But there was more as well, wasn't there? Did you relate to the person at a social level? Did you feel welcome in the room? Were all your questions answered? Was there a direct, one-on-one exchange at a point or at points during the class that left upon you a particularly positive or negative impression of the instructor?

This list of questions could go on and on (it may feel as if it already has); the point being that the list of impressions and questions could be quite lengthy. The challenge, then, is how to capture the most major elements of your reaction to the program about which you are reflecting. The traditional method is to give you a list of questions for you to react to by assigning rating values to each item. From there, the numbers provided are averaged, and that single number is taken as the assignment of value or feeling you have about the program. So let's review:

- The survey designer wants to know how you feel overall about a training experience.
- To find this out, the designer develops as many questions about individual elements that made up

the experience as possible (knowing he or she probably missed some).

- Each one of these elements requires you to assign some sort of rating or score value (e.g., rate the instructor's eye contact, rate the voice quality of the instructor, rate how well your questions were answered, etc.).
- In that it is impossible to know which elements are more important to you than others, each of the ratings is considered of equal importance, summed, and averaged.
- The resulting number is supposed to be the "value" you put on the program.
- End result: a survey that contains twenty to thirty items, which associate with some numeric values, which are in turn averaged into a single value, which is then supposed to represent how you feel.

I think I can offer an alternative. Rather than putting together twenty to thirty questions along with some arbitrary numeric rating scale to approximate what you thought of a program, I might use this question: "Would you say that the program was valuable to you?"

To which you could respond with one of these answers:

a) "I did not value it much at all."
b) "I saw some limited value."
c) "I think the program was valuable."
d) "I think the program was of tremendous value."

Hmmm-m-m. I am going out on a limb here; I would guess that you'd feel that I would capture how you really felt better with one question than by tiring you out by asking you to rate twenty to thirty items and averaging them into some numeric value, which might have different meanings to different people. Am I right? I am also going to guess that the rating that you give to me using my one question would remain more consistent over time than if I asked you the same twenty to thirty questions at intervals over the upcoming years. I am going to guess that you would not remember today how good the instructor's eye contact was, even if you sat in the class last week, let alone if you are reflecting on a class you took three years ago. However, I bet that the feelings you had about the class three years ago are about the same feelings that you had about the class today. That's just one of those funny things about being a sentient being — feelings last, even if details become blurred. Kind of makes you wonder what your dog really thinks of you since that time he stared at you getting out of the shower a couple of years back, doesn't it?

Keep It Light, Will Ya?

There will be elements of this section that relate to the section on conversational language. This is a separate concept though, and an important one. That's why the two sections are separated from each other.

There is no way in the world that we will ever be able to design a survey or assessment that has no effect on the person participating. (That is the observer effect I mentioned in chapter 5.) Because there will be an influence on the respondent one way or another and our objective is to get the best response rate possible, it makes sense that we want to keep the tone light and positive.

To give an example, if you go into work on Monday and see a fellow worker to whom you say something inane and harmless like, "So how was your weekend?" would you rather hear, "Very nice—went with the family to the beach—had a blast—how about you?" or would you prefer, "Oh my gawd! If you only knew . . . it had to be one of the most boring weekends of my life! Let me tell you all about it . . ."?

Now let's change this up some. This time you are asking questions on a health assessment. (Just so that you know, the "Standard Health Question Style" on the left side of the table is a real survey excerpt actually used by licensed physicians.) Both sets of question items are to be answered "yes" or "no." Which do you think will get more active participation while affecting the answers the least?

Standard Health Question Style	The "Upbeat" Style
I often feel lonely even when I am with other people.	I am seldom lonely even when I am alone.
It is difficult for me to make friends.	I make friends about as easily as most.
I lack confidence.	I feel confident in most normal situations.
I often feel very tense.	I usually am at ease during the day.
It takes a lot of effort for me to do simple tasks.	I am able to accomplish most tasks I need to with ease.
I feel a strong need to sleep during the day.	Most days I feel fairly rested and alert.

Trust me on this: Both sets of items have a "binary re-sponse format," which is psychologist talk for pick one of two answers; either you relate to what is stated, or you don't. If someone was really going to say, "Yes! That's me!" to *any* of the items on the left side, you can be sure they would say "no" to the equivalent items on the right side. The only difference is that after you get done with the ques-tions on the left, you probably start to feel bad and perhaps regret taking the assessment. On the other hand, the items on the right have a tendency to make you feel energized. You would most likely not mind answering similar ques-tions in the future. I have to wonder who decided that science and medicine had to be gloomy to be valid.

Assess and Measure Feelings, Not Judgments

There is going to be an entire chapter that builds on this point, so we won't spend a whole lot of time on it right now. It is important that you understand a couple of preliminary points here anyway as it relates to response ratios and survey completion rates.

First, the human mind is divided into two hemi-spheres, the left and right "brain," if you will. The science of brain function still has a way to go until we really have a handle on how all that gray matter works to do all that it does, but it is generally accepted[16] that the "left brain" is

---

[16] By "generally accepted," I mean accepted more completely than is actually supported by scientific research. There is way too much oversimplification of the functions of either hemisphere of the brain and there are fairly high percentages of people whose brain func-tions, in some respects anyway, are the *opposite* of popular belief. That having been said, I am going to exploit popular misunderstand-ing with reckless abandon . . .

our logical, analytical, numeric side and the "right brain" is the language-based, intuitive, creative, feeling side.

The problem with most surveys and assessments is that they, at best, ask about reactions and feelings — but then ask that we assign a numeric value to those feelings. That is a bit tough to do — "on a scale from one to ten, how pretty is this flower?" Worse yet are those surveys where we as laypeople are asked to evaluate or judge some quality or behavior that can only really be assessed by a trained expert. That is the type of question like "Was the instructor knowledgeable?" C'mon! If I knew enough about database programming to know if the instructor was knowledgeable about database programming, I wouldn't be taking the class! (Duh!)

The second point is that even though we act like good soldiers and answer questions that use these dumb numeric scales, we end up making repeated mental shifts between the brain hemispheres. In other words, we use the right hemisphere to react to the flower or sunset at an emotional, holistic level, and then struggle to translate the feeling into a number using the left hemisphere of the brain. It is a clunky mental activity at best, and one we are not really designed to handle well. That is why, with most surveys that use those rat-

The sunsets were pretty.
1 = strongly disagree and 5 = strongly agree

those rating scales, you start to find your eyes crossing after about the third or fourth item and just want to mark everything a "four." It is like running along a river bank and repeatedly jumping from one side to the other along the way—even if you start out strong, pretty soon you are going to get your pants wet.

Summary

That's about it for this chapter. Hopefully it exposed you to some new ways of looking at your fellow sentient beings, the way we think and process, and maybe gave you a few ideas as to how to bring your survey response rates up to more acceptable levels. These concepts, although basic, are fundamental to assessment success and will be carried forward as we delve yet further into the science of finding out stuff.

Chapter 8: *Preparing Your Respondents*

Ranking right up there with an unexpected visit from distant relatives or an unexpected work assignment with a very short fuse is the impromptu survey or evaluation you discover in your email inbox. You know, the one that reads:

Dear Team Member:

As part of our ongoing efforts to improve performance of our staff, we are evaluating the leadership skills of selected managers. You have been selected to rate the performance of [name of some manager] on 367 key indicators. Please take a few minutes to complete the survey by clicking on the following link:
www.longandboringquestions.com/survey88H56/ABC

Your participation is critical and we need to have you submit the survey by close of business tomorrow.

Thanks for your help!

Regards,
The BOSS.

With a blend of feelings including suspicion, frustration, and confusion, you tentatively click on the URL to find yourself in a position of rating somebody you sort of know on the aforementioned 367 traits and behaviors that may only be known to that somebody's mother and possibly significant "other."

Things like:

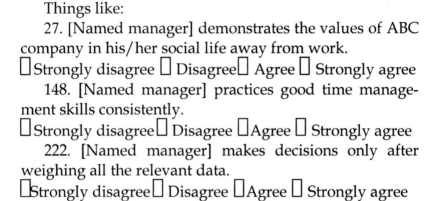

27. [Named manager] demonstrates the values of ABC company in his/her social life away from work.
☐ Strongly disagree ☐ Disagree☐ Agree ☐ Strongly agree

148. [Named manager] practices good time management skills consistently.
☐ Strongly disagree☐ Disagree ☐Agree ☐ Strongly agree

222. [Named manager] makes decisions only after weighing all the relevant data.
☐ Strongly disagree☐ Disagree ☐Agree ☐ Strongly agree

In that you have only brief, albeit frequent interactions with this person and wish her/him no harm, you probably do what most of us do, which is to strain to think of any supporting evidence to justify all the "agree" responses you are assigning. Unfortunately, you haven't really given a lot of thought to how the rated person thinks or acts—what if this person is really a stellar performer and you are rating him too low? What if she/he is a serial killer and you are making him or her out to be some sort of role model? Events like this take place all year, every year, at thousands of work locations across the country and the globe. I think of them as "drive-by" assessments because they seem to hit unsuspecting people with a terrifying randomness of which none of us is exempt if we work in places where others regularly gather.

There are a few fundamental flaws in this time-honored approach to assessing human performance:

1. The raters were probably not prepared to render an informed opinion.
2. Even if they were prepared, nobody determined if the raters were willing.

3. And if they were willing, the assessment design was so loosely constructed and administered that finding truly valid results was probably impossible.
4. Finally, who says the people being assessed even wanted to hear about the opinions?

In short, we have another case of the unwilling being led by the unknowing striving to do the impossible for the ungrateful. Let's see if we can do something about this. After all, we have been doing so much with so little for so long, we are probably ready now to do anything with nothing.[17]

The Raters are Unprepared (And Perhaps Not All That Willing)

I have a lot of confidence in my fellow humans, particularly in their collective opinions—if I have reason to believe that they formed their opinions based on their own experiences and reactions. With a few arguable exceptions, [18] the American populace has made fairly good Presidential selections considering the field from which they had to choose. Continuing to use national elections as an example, think how much "consideration time" one has regarding for whom she or he will vote. There are volumes of information about the candidates available for review, not to mention opportunities to see

[17] This concept was stolen. If you are old enough to remember the Vietnam War, you might have heard a variation of this or read it somewhere. I couldn't find anyone to attribute it to. Some people attribute it to Mother Theresa, but that just doesn't sound right. I think it was just one of those catchy quotes that popped up during the 1960s (as far as I know). It sure works here though . . .
[18] I was making reference to Andrew Johnson and Warren G. Harding—to whom did *you* think I was referring?

review, not to mention opportunities to see and hear the candidates themselves. Then, best of all, voting is voluntary, actual votes are anonymous, and the results are aggregated. In most cases, by aggregating the votes, every stupid choice is cancelled out by a smart one with (hopefully) a few smart voting choices left over to carry the day. What a country!

The same generous allotment of time and information doesn't happen with internal corporate assessments and surveys, especially the ones used for "professional development." Those are the multi-rater assessments that are used to identify strengths and weaknesses of individuals based on the feedback provided by a few contemporaries. In those cases, generally between three and seven people are selected by some means to evaluate the behavior and performance of another individual. Those three to seven people are (strongly) encouraged to rate one individual on a

> If a survey is important enough to put together in the first place and important enough to use as the basis for decisions, certainly it is important enough to give your respondents (the raters) the opportunity to do a good job.

plethora of granular issues thought to, in combination, paint a picture of leadership performance, communication skill, or some other behavior or trait. And the raters are not given much time to gather information upon which to base their ratings either. The same issues of granularity of topic and limited time to prepare thoughtful responses apply in general to most organizational surveys and assessments.

The solution is as straightforward as it is obvious: give people the time to understand what they are being asked and the time to gather sufficient information to be able to answer. If a survey is important enough to put together in the first place and important enough to use as the basis for decisions, certainly it is important enough to give your respondents (the raters) the opportunity to do a good job. If it is worth the effort in a presidential election, I would think it would be worth it to improve the quality of your organizational leadership. Think about it—who really affects your life more directly and intimately—the president of the U.S. or one of your managers at work? (If you are reading this in your current capacity as White House Chief of Staff, this last point may be confusing because the president IS your manager at work—if this is the case, call me and I will clear it up for you.)

So how do we do it? Again, it is fairly simple. Once the assessment is designed to your specific requirements, publish it to the potential pool of raters as well as subjects being rated. Encourage people to look the survey over. It is not a classified document (again, if you are the White House Chief of Staff, *really* the assessment is not a classified document . . .). This gives people an opportunity to understand what is being asked and measured by the instrument. They become comfortable with the idea of watching for the specific behaviors rather than just being slapped with a series of questions requiring an instant response. The subjects being rated get a little more comfortable with the behavioral questions as well.

Let's review:

- Design the instrument with a "time cushion" built in before formal release of the assessment (there is no definitive time frame; probably give people a week or two).

- Use the time cushion period to permit a pre-administration release of the questions to potential raters and subjects so everyone is familiar with the content, direction, and purpose. (It doesn't hurt to send email[s] to encourage discussion about the survey either—keep it open and top of mind for people.)
- From the pool of potential raters, take steps to identify those who would be available and willing to give the assessment the time and energy required. Ask for volunteers if need be—create a list of possible names—even create a simple contest or drawing out of the event to gain interest.)
- Encourage discussion about the content of the instrument so that people become focused on the data that will be required (at staff meetings, through emails, etc.).
- Once the interested raters are identified (using the above techniques), initiate the assessment process.

By taking those extra steps, we will have largely eliminated the "unknowing" and "unwilling" from the equation.

Assessment Construction
Other chapters deal more completely with the technical issues surrounding assessments but a few basic concepts need to be mentioned here.

- The average respondent's interest in completion of a survey diminishes slightly after the first ten items.

96

- The average respondent's interest in completion of a survey clearly diminishes after the first twenty items.

- The average respondent's interest in completion of a survey diminishes rapidly and significantly after the first thirty items.

- After the first fifty items, unless you are providing some sort of entertainment value to the respondent, the care and interest in the responses given is virtually non-existent.

- After one hundred items, the respondent is ticked off and looking for the <ESC> key on the computer.

I know that sometimes it is impossible to ask all you want to ask in just a few questions. I have myself even created assessments that number in the hundreds of items. But believe me,

> After 100 items, the respondent is ticked off and looking for the <ESC> key on the computer.

when I had to release an assessment of that length, I took heroic measures to ensure that respondents were made as comfortable as possible with the assessment—things like allowing stops and returns to online surveys. I included completion thermometers at the top of each page to provide a sense of accomplishment. I changed up the way the items looked and how responses were recorded. I also went to great lengths to advise the respondents as to the length going in and thanking them profusely for making the attempt. I don't know how much it helped, but I made the gesture. You should do the same. And before you decide that an item or question really needs to be included, please ask yourself the following questions:

- Can I reasonably expect that the respondent will be able to answer this fairly and honestly based on only moderate interest in the subject?
- Will the data that I get from this item really help answer the fundamental questions that created the need for the assessment in the first place?

If you don't hear yourself saying "yes" to both questions, you might do well to bag the question item. I think you get the idea—too many questions can be worse than too few. With too few, you may wonder what else you might have discovered. With too many, you have to wonder which answers are genuine and which were given just to get the thing over with. In other words, would you rather have *no* information or *wrong* information if you were going to make a decision? (The credited response to that question is that no information is better than wrong information—if you don't believe me, just ask the White House Chief of Staff.)

So Who Wants to Know?

This may be the shortest section of the entire book. Just be sure that the data you are collecting is going to be used in a positive way by somebody. Avoid using surveys or assessments as a tool to justify doing something unpleasant to somebody else (passing over for a raise, staff cut-backs, ending programs, etc.). Once word gets out that your surveys are going to be used to do anything other than positively benefit people, the odds of you getting genuine, honest responses starts falling somewhere between slim and none.

There you have it—we have eliminated the possibility that you will unknowingly recruit a crowd of unwilling folks to complete an impossible task for a bunch of ingrates . . . insofar as internal performance assessments are concerned, anyway. You are on your own with your other job duties.

Chapter 9: *Assessment Is a Process, Not an Event*

For those of you working in organizations of even moderate size, this chapter is going to be both valuable and challenging. Valuable, because many of the ideas we have covered previously are given a framework for implementation in this chapter. Challenging, because you are probably part of an organization of at least moderate size—this in turn means there is going to be resistance to change simply *because* it represents a change. Change is traditionally difficult for organizations. If you choose to accept the challenge, remember that previously accepted concepts have eventually gone by the wayside. I have provided a few examples below that should help you keep your faith that change is possible—for the longest time, people believed these things; they were just part of life:

> "If man were meant to fly, he would have been born with wings."
> "The earth is the center of the solar system; the sun, moon, and planets revolve around Earth."
> "You will stay cross-eyed if you cross your eyes long enough."
> "It takes seven years to digest gum."

As you are now aware, I occasionally like to deviate from the central topic to share an interesting note or observation. In this case, what appears to be a digression is actually a point of emphasis. It is about Mike, the Headless Wonder Chicken (pictures below).

The "Headless Wonder Chicken" lived for 18 months without a head

I mention Mike because in my research on myths and misconceptions that have persisted over time, I discovered that there are those who to this day question Mike's longevity (eighteen months with no head). Some things, albeit uncomfortable to accept, are nevertheless true. So as informed adults, we have to accept both perspectives that (1) some dumb ideas need to be retired, and (2) some ideas that seem to be a bit difficult to accept might in fact be true. If you find that your initial attempts to implement a better way to measure and assess are met with some skepticism, remember all that Mike went through.

A Quick Review of Concepts

We have covered a lot of ground in the first chapters and because it is good stuff, we can benefit from a brief review before charging forward. Here is an encore of some relevant key principles and concepts:

- Most "backward" or past-focused assessments (which is just about everything in existence), including training ROI, "smiley sheets," and end-of-course examinations, are of little practical value for planning purposes—it is kind of like driving a car by using the rear-view mirror rather than looking through the windshield.

- Any measurement or rating system, no matter how perfectly constructed, can be rendered worthless in the hands of an incompetent rater. Conclusions drawn from such administrations are therefore invalid. Make sure the people completing your assessments and surveys are willing and able to give you information you can use.

- When we measure training outcomes or behavior changes, we affect those outcomes; this can be used to our advantage if we are crafty.

- If you want measurement to influence the outcome of the process you are measuring positively, you need to measure outcomes during the event process—only current and timely measurements provide completely actionable information.

- Most people feel they have better things to do than to answer questions. However, most people also think they are smarter than you are. If asked properly, they will tell you all about themselves and their world in hopes of impressing you with their insight and wisdom.

Heady stuff, isn't it? Anyway, here is a trick to make it all come together for the benefit of everyone: ***these concepts (and therefore assessments and surveys) have to be applied early and often.*** Sorry, but there is no way around this. If you do a bunch of things in your organization intended to change how people behave, you will have to serve up a bunch of assessments to figure out how it is going and to get actionable information.

I can almost hear it now — "Survey fatigue!" "No time!" "They won't like this!" "They'll never go for it!" "If man were meant to fly, he would have been born with wings!" "Yada, yada, yada!" Let's take a look at how to make it happen anyway.

You Are Asking People to Complete Some Surveys — You Aren't Asking Them to Shampoo a Porcupine

People don't like doing things they consider extra work or trouble. But if we can put this requirement in perspective, we can eventually get reasonable buy-in. Completion of a survey is in many respects much less trouble and aggravation than por- cupine shampooing, for example.

Appropriate porcupine-shampooing requires putting safety first.

In fact, it is less ag- gravating than many things we do almost every day. Think about it in relative terms.

Please rank these common, everyday occurrences in order of their irritation quotient — put a number "1" next to the most onerous, a "2" next to the next worst, all the way through "10," the least unpleasant of possible events in your day:

____ Driving to/from work in rush-hour traffic

____ Waiting on hold/working through telephone "trees"

____ Listening to excuses for why something you needed wasn't done or done correctly

____ Watching most television commercials

_____ Opening little plastic packages of either ketchup or chips

_____Surly customer service people who wish you would go away

_____People on cell phones in cars and restaurants who forget there is anyone else around

_____Sitting in rooms that are too cold, too hot, too humid or where you get static electricity shocks every time you touch something metal

_____Forgetting your user ID or password because you couldn't have the one you easily remember and use on most of the other sites

_____Having to reload the copier with paper to print two pages

You could probably add a few aggravations of your own. The point is, relative to *this* list of ranked aggravations, where would a brief, entertaining, and engaging survey end up? (And, by the way, you just participated in a survey right here. Did it bother you a lot?)

Do You Mean to Tell Me . . . ?

The second argument supporting the idea of asking people who went to a training program or people who are experiencing some major corporate change to complete multiple surveys is based in economics. Or, put another way, do you mean to tell me that your organization is willing to invest several thousands (or tens of thousands) of dollars in a training program (or similar amounts in some reorganization) *without* bothering to spend a fraction of the time and money to see what the outcomes are?

Let's assume you are of the means and inclination to give a friend or relative a costly gift, like an all-expenses-

paid cruise or a fine, luxury automobile. Would you figure that your gesture was appreciated and let it go at
that? Or would you want a little feedback as to how the
gift was received, what the experience was like, and if
there were any issues (good or bad) that affected the experience? I am guessing you would probably welcome the
feedback. (And I personally would welcome you as my
friend if you do typically give gifts like that— but I digress . . .)

From a business perspective, is there any less logic in
finding out the details of the ongoing effects of training or
organizational change initiatives? Is it not really your *obligation* to gather such information as part of performing
due diligence around the outcomes of the behavioral intervention?

In summary, well-designed surveys and assessments
are simply not all that time consuming or unpleasant to
complete. But even if they were, it seems reasonable to
look into the effects of your organization's investment just
to see if you poured money down the rat hole—huge concern about whether respondents will enjoy the experience
of giving feedback seems somewhat unwarranted. This is
especially true if they had little or no choice about attending the training or enduring the change initiative. Why all
the concern at this point?

The Nuts and Bolts of the Process—Some Handy Tips
Up to this point, we have discussed the possible reactions to the idea of conducting regular assessments. Next,
we attempted to provide some arguments as to why it is
important work. I figure that, somewhere along the way, I

may have persuaded you to implement an effective measurement strategy. If so, I should offer some basic ideas of how to put it into place. The ideas below are just suggestions. Feel free to steal the ideas and modify them to your own advantage. Heaven knows, I have made a career out of such behavior.

Start Building Your Library

Once you have a survey or assessment that is working, not only should you celebrate your success, you should make efforts to keep a copy of the items on file (physically, or better yet, electronically) so that you can pull them out as needed for future projects. You will want to classify the forms or the items in the forms for future reference, but it has been my experience that too much effort in coding and classifying items ends up becoming an administrative nightmare. I would recommend that your classifying consist of just three tags at the form (not item) level:

- Month and year it was first used
- What program it was used for
- What kind of information you got out of it (e.g., knowledge recall? Reactions to the program? Behavior change estimates?)

I once worked for an organization that set off on a mission to classify every survey item currently in use by the organization. That's right—I said *every survey item*, not every survey or assessment as a whole. Wait though—it gets better. Not only were we to identify every discrete item in use (near as I can tell that would represent probably 10,000+ questions), each was to be classified and coded with several unique "tags" for use in a relational database. The tags represented things like this:

- The way the item was worded (was it a question or a statement?)
- Response mechanism associated with each item (1–5 scale, check box, drop down list, multiple choice single answer, multiple choice/multiple answer, etc., etc.)With what program or initiative was it associated? (One of several hundred training classes? An internal initiative? Some sort of needs analysis? Etc, etc.)
- What was it actually measuring? (Opinion? Knowledge? Attitude/value? An estimate of change?)

I know in my heart of hearts there were other tags that were to be recorded and tracked, but one of the merciful effects of time is that many past idiocies are eventually forgotten. Nevertheless, even considering the tags and volume of items as presented here, the task was so gargantuan as to make its completion very unlikely. This project was one of several "innovations" that a senior executive supposedly wanted to see implemented. In her case, she really did not want anything to happen

> She really did not want anything to happen and figured that if it became unwieldy enough, it would eventually be abandoned while helping her achieve her goal of appearing to be a global thinker. . .

and figured that if it became unwieldy enough, it would eventually be abandoned while helping her achieve her goal of appearing to be a global thinker and innovator. If you are serious about making an assessment strategy a part of your organization to be used as a valuable planning device, keep the process simple. A library of assessments of reasonable size can be a time saver.

Start Building Expectations

As we discussed at the beginning of the chapter, people don't often like changes. But in the grand scheme of life, there are many things that we don't much like but that are good for us, and an integrated assessment process is one of those "good for us" things. All you need to do is to plan on letting everyone concerned know that feedback is needed and appreciated at your organization. Then tell them that as part of collecting that valued feedback, they should expect to see an increase in the number of surveys and assessments they will be asked to complete. Ideally, you will have the blessing of a senior executive (preferably one who is liked and respected, but one who is feared will work almost as well). This blessing will consist of a memorandum or two or maybe a mention at significant staff meetings of the expectation that people will respond to the surveys. In your organization, leadership probably has preferred methods of getting general communication out to everyone. It is best to use this favored method to reach your population as well.

From there, you simply start ramping up the number and frequency of surveys. At first, there may be some grumbling, but it should soon die down. Realistically, surveys are not so onerous that people can muster up that much resentment about them, and before you know it, it will become a part of the "culture" of your organization. Should there be persistent resistance to the new assessment strategy, you can always poll the employee population to find out what it is that they so dislike about being polled. You may find a great solution to the problem. (And you thought I was joking.)

Keep the Process Engaging

People have a tendency to support any process for which they feel involved and for which they see results. This is accomplished by giving feedback in the form of letting the respondents know how the surveys and assessments turned out. Questions you might consider answering for respondents include:

- What was discovered?
- What changes will take place as a result of the feedback?
- What good has come out of the information gleaned from the respondents?

When people find that they are listened to, they tend to offer more information when asked. You can view this process as a marketing effort, which can be supported through regular email updates or newsletter stories in the corporate intranet site. Your organization probably has an internal communication mechanism of one sort or another. Just integrate assessment news as part of the process.

A True-Life Story

Lest you think this is just pie-in-the-sky theory, let me share a real life example of how well this strategy can work. I have worked with several clients who have had good success in implementing survey strategies — remember this is just one story.

I worked with a medium-sized financial organization that had grown through aggressive leadership and acquisition. As a result of its rapid growth, there were effectively management headquarters in two states, one in the East and one in the Western U.S. Of course there were regional offices sprinkled all over the country, adding to the complexity of communication and coordination. The company decided that in order to perpetuate its growth, leaders had to refine skills and mid-level management had to be groomed for greater responsibility. The beauty of the training program was found in the attitude of the executive leadership and managers. They knew there was room for improvement and they were willing to accept whatever feedback would guide them.

They underwent an extensive leadership program involving nearly one hundred mid-level to senior managers from across the country, which addressed everything from interpersonal communication to creating and expressing a dynamic vision to guide the organization. The program was done in three phases over the course of about fifteen months. Feedback about the training, the reactions of direct reports, estimates of what behavioral changes they were going to make individually, and more were all assessed at 1–2 month intervals and reported back to the executive team. This is where it gets good. Instead of just keeping the feedback inside the executive suite, the leadership team made *all* the feedback public to *all* the staff via broadcast emails with reports attached (that was their routine way of linking all the offices together when general information was to be disseminated). It did not matter whether the reports were positive or corrective in nature. Their attitude was, "We did what we did and got what we got—now how can we make it better?"

At first, I got reports from the training staff that people did not really know what to do with the summary feedback report about their feedback. It was not that they were in any way upset by getting specific news of what the collective effort was producing—they just had not expected to hear anything back at all from their input. Inside of four months (about 2–3 reporting cycles) several things happened:

- Emails were being sent to me, as the measurement consultant *outside of the organization*, which included questions about specific performance measures they thought would be of value that I should incorporate in future assessments.
- I also would field questions as to when the next report was due to be released because respondents were interested in how their personal opinions matched up against the aggregate findings.
- As time went on, I would see comments on the forms that referenced the positive changes that were occurring. Here is a sample of actual quotes that appeared on the forms:
  - "I saw a difference almost immediately when he returned from training; this reporting is a great help for his development and for his team . . ."
  - "The survey itself does a good job of covering basic aspects in the work setting . . ."
  - "There has been a noticeable increase in effort by ***** in the last 45–60 days[19] to motivate and help others achieve the goals of the company by

---

[19] This was the typical period between reports at this organization.

training staff and by his own professional example."

o "***** is an overall supportive manager. I feel that the area for most improvement is in understanding individual transactions and our program more thoroughly. It is evident that ******* is taking the appropriate steps to improve this aspect of his leadership ability. Kudos."

o " . . . We are on the right track!"

I am happy to report that the policy of regularly collecting and sharing information continued with significant success. Your organization's story may be slightly different but if you can garner the support of your leadership to create a two-way communication about assessment outcomes, I would expect that your results would be similar.

In Conclusion—How Do You Eat an Elephant?

There is little to add—implementing an assessment strategy in your organization simply requires a single-minded intention to do so. Once it is started, if the principles in the rest of this book are applied, the process will soon take on a life of its own and everyone will be better off for it. It is kind of like starting a fitness program or keeping a New Year's resolution—or eating an elephant; you succeed by taking things one step (or bite) at a time.

Chapter 10: *The Outcome of Effort (OOE) Model: Predict, Verify, and Validate*

Several chapters ago we discussed the Uncertainty Principle (which was really the Observer Effect as applied to training assessment). If you remember the underlying concepts, give yourself a gold star for good reading comprehension and retention. Just in case you are a bit fuzzy in the recall department, here are some key points that serve as the foundation for what is going to come next:

- Openly measuring behaviors and performance causes the subjects to be focused on the behaviors being measured.
- When you openly acknowledge that you intend to make specific behavior changes, there is a greater motivation to follow through than if you did not acknowledge your intent.
- Individuals are aware of their own deliberate behavior changes and the effects of those changes earlier than anyone else.
- If you want to have third parties accurately observe and validate behavior changes in others, you will need to give them notice of what they are to be looking for well in advance of the formal validation process.

This chapter is about the real-world application of some of the principles. It is kind of a do-it-yourself guide to administration of the Outcome of Effort Model. To make it more memorable and to indulge my incessant need for silliness, I have been getting people to refer to it as the OOE (pronounced oooh-wee—as in, "Oooh-wee! The executives are actually taking training seriously for a change!"). The strength of this model is that it is what statisticians would call robustness—it has tremendous flexibility in terms of its administration to meet a variety of conditions. As we go through the model, I will share with you the places that you can change things up a little without losing the benefits.

A Very Brief History

The development of the OOE Model came out of the need to have something to satisfy the request of senior level leaders to provide "training ROI" analysis. If you recall, training ROI is kind of an interesting animal. On the surface, it has elements that seem to make sense in terms of evaluating the benefits of a training program. In reality, it is quite a stretch to translate an expense into investment terms and to measure accurately and consistently what a training program delivered. That is part of the reason the concept has been around for years while only about 5 percent of companies ever really do ROI analysis—that's opposed to over 80 percent that regularly do end-of-course satisfaction surveys (smiley sheets)[20].

---

[20] Why the comparison of the lofty training ROI to the humble end of course survey? Research has shown that the information theoretically obtained by each type of assessment is valued equally by businesses (each type of measurement was valued by 43% of those responding). The businesses responded to a checklist of assessments in response to the question, "What measures are most valuable?" – for more details, see J. Bersin, *High-Impact Learning Measurement: Best*

My research suggested that what most everyone wanted in terms of a comprehensive analysis was not so much to find out what a program cost. Rather, they wanted to know what behaviors were changed on the job and whether the organization's business strategies were being carried out. That is analogous to the difference between figuring out how much it cost to drive to the store versus determining if the store had stuff you needed when you got there. It is really a moot point to discover that you can save $4.93 in gas using one vehicle rather than another, if you drive thirty-five miles only to discover they aren't carrying your pet iguana's favorite treat (which, by the way, is a wild plum-like fruit from the *Spondias monbin* [Hog Plum] tree . . . pardon the digression if you already knew that).

To identify behaviors accurately, you really have to observe actions over time and under a variety of circumstances until a pattern emerges. This means that observations, or more precisely, *reports* of observations, have to be made as behaviors are practiced. That means that any assessments have to be spaced out over long enough periods so that habits can be formed and practiced. Time also allows for even casual observers to see changes in others then.

Last, I spent some time deciding what the stakeholders in a training intervention process really wanted when they talked about measurements—I came up with the following:

Practices, Models, and Business-Driven Solutions for the Measurement and Evaluation of Corporate Training 2006, (Bersin & Associates: 11 November: 2006), PDF.

- Reports that are understandable
- Reports that contain information that is not already known
- Reports that provide information that people can act on
- Ideally, the act of getting the information for the reports helps support the training intervention

It is worth mentioning here again that people don't really want assessments or measurements—they want the *information* that the assessments provide. Our focus always has to be on the final goal of providing usable (actionable) information.

With those assumptions in place, I set out to create a system that could address these issues (below):

The OOE Model

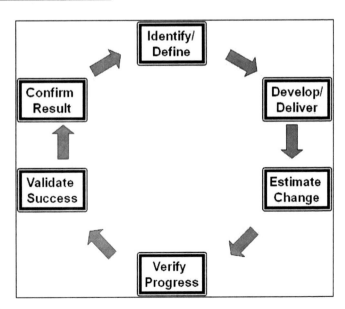

There you have it. Perhaps a little explanation is in order . . .

Phase 1: Identify/Define

This first phase is intended to address several questions. The first question is easy: Why do we train anybody in anything? (To change behaviors.) The rest of the questions are kind of lumped together and will be answered all at once:

- What behaviors should we change then?
- What will things look like when the new behaviors are in place?
- Why do we think the behaviors will help? (In other words, what do we want to accomplish in terms of business outcomes?)
- What does success look like from a business perspective?
- What measures will we use to measure that success?

The answer is that there has to be a link between behaviors and desired business outcomes. For example, let's say that we want to diversify our sales pipeline to promote steady sales growth.

- The objective is to provide for steady sales growth.
- The interim success is to increase the volume and diversity in the pipeline.
- The behavior believed to make it happen is to increase the actual number of cold calls in a week.
- The training is intended to prepare sales people to manage their time and to optimize their success with cold calls.

119

By making this "roadmap," if you will, we are linking the training to observable, measurable behaviors, which in turn link to interim business results, which fold into the business objective—everything is in alignment.

Let's look at the Guiding Triangle Model from chapter 1 again:

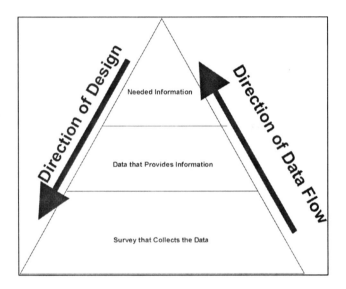

This process is started with an interview procedure done by the training department or whoever is charged with the responsibility of putting together a program. The interview is conducted with the stakeholder who wants the change in the first place, to make sure there is a clear outcome defined. All too frequently, a leader has a vague idea of what she or he wants to see happen and just assumes the details will take care of themselves. This is a potential problem. When things work out differently than imagined, there is plenty of room to blame the program developers or the people going through the intervention, when the real problem was that the original idea was not fleshed out sufficiently to create an accurate goal or vision.

We see this failure to take proper planning steps all the time in other areas:

- The ridiculously high divorce rate in the U.S.
- The Iraqi War
- Low use of HOV (diamond lanes) on otherwise strangled freeways
- Automotive, toy, drug, and food recalls
- The purchase of measurement books other than this one

These travesties can often be avoided with proper planning and execution. To help with that, this first phase was built on three rules of measurement:

- If an outcome, attitude, or opinion can be described in behavioral terms, it can be measured.
- If any outcome, attitude, or opinion cannot be described in behavioral terms, it cannot be measured.
- The greatest challenge in measurement is framing an outcome in behavioral terms.

Phase 2: Develop/Deliver

The process actually starts to get a little easier from this point forward, because we have a strong foundation and direction. It can apply to promoting a corporate change initiative or to regular training. The approach is similar for either process, so I choose to continue with my sales training scenario. Here we address some of the critical training design/selection issues.

Whether you are designing in-house training or using an outside vendor, you want to make sure that the training being presented is in alignment with the business outcomes. In our earlier example, the training would need to address cold calls and proper use of time to optimize the results desired. Every good training program has learning objectives — what we need to do is condition ourselves to think of the learning objectives as being successful when we have started to change *behaviors* to meet the business objectives. Again, using our example, we want to make our participants more effective and efficient with making cold calls that ultimately get prospects into the pipeline.

Finally, we want to figure out how to measure the behavioral changes that will occur. This is very important — if behaviors change, but we can't identify them for reporting purposes, we won't know how well we are succeeding until much later.

In summary, the deliverable from this phase is a well written and presented program or initiative. But just as importantly, the design and approach has built-in objectives that allow for meaningful measurement of the effects. This leads us to another key point — our measures have to be easily converted into reports that everybody can understand. It doesn't do us much good if we take measurements that are overly complex and involved. Often people spend a great deal of time collecting tons of information with no particular thought as to how to compile it into a readable report. The goal is K.I.S.S. (Keep It Simple, Sweetheart) — get data that is easy to record, manipulate, and report.

Phase 3: Estimate Change

Here is where things get interesting, because until OOE, there has been only limited application of the principles in this book to assessment practice.

Assessment and measurement has evolved from measurements taken about processes happening on the factory floor or in laboratories then ultimately moved into the human domain. The change estimate (prediction) phase is part of what makes the OOE model uniquely applicable to human endeavors. There was never any real need to make predictions about "widget" production—it was a simple arithmetic estimate. If a machine was supposed to produce five hundred widgets in an hour and you wanted to know how many widgets would be produced by the end of an eight-hour day, all you had to do was some simple multiplication and you had your prediction. Because people are not widgets, this type of approach won't work. Think about it— people and organizations are not especially predictable; they TEND to demonstrate certain behaviors, but they are influenced by lots of factors. That makes prediction imprecise—a problem unrelated to manufacturing, and therefore not much considered—UNTIL NOW. For business to survive and prosper nowadays, we need to make the best predictions we can. It is no longer okay to wait to see what happens with the people in our organizations.

These are some steps that make for a good OOE model predictive assessment:

- Give the assessment soon after the training (or kick-off meeting, etc.) ends (about 1–3 days later).

- The issues you should address include questions about what changes will be occurring, what observable behaviors will be different, and how information will be applied; you can ask more but include these topics for sure.
- Be sure to ask what barriers to success may exist and be ready to take action on the information that you get from the assessment.
- Process the data as rapidly as possible (close the assessment within seven days and start doing the analysis and reporting).
- Be sure to report out the results as widely as you can — people love to know that they have been heard.

Remember, these assessments are designed to be robust and flexible. You can create questions that are important to you. Please consider the sample below to be possible ideas — not suggestions. You can easily create your own based on the behavioral objectives that came out of the first two phases.

The training will help me to better plan my sales calls.
☐ I would not say that ☐ Maybe some, but not much
☐ True, it will ☐ It will make a big difference

The training program is going to help me increase the average size of my sale.
☐ I would not say that ☐ Maybe some, but not much
☐ True, it will ☐ It will make a big difference

I learned several new techniques to make my calls more productive for both the client and for myself.
☐ I would not say that ☐ I learned one or two skills
☐ True ☐ They will make me *much* more effective

What three things do you best remember from the training?

1._____

2._____

3._____

Sales Effectiveness

☐ Actual numbers will be improved (larger sales, more sales, etc.).

☐ There will likely be less time spent in "re-selling" to existing clients.

☐ I expect there will be less loss of business to the competition.

☐ People will feel more comfortable in sharing information about their requirements to help me address needs.

Please tell us about anything that may present a barrier to your success. (You may remain anonymous—we just need to know what to improve.)

Final tip: Whenever reasonable, limit the number of questions to fewer than twenty-five with just a few open-ended responses. You will get a much higher response rate if you keep things fairly brief and positive.

Verify Progress

As we said earlier, prediction of outcomes that involve human nature are not perfect—attitudes change, unexpected things happen. That makes this verification phase an important one. It is your chance to see just how things are going in the "real world" and to make changes if needed. Typically, gathering this information is as easy as a quick online survey about forty-five days out, but other methods, like focus groups or telephone surveys, can be used if the situation requires it. This is your first opportunity following the prediction stage to get feedback as to "How" (as Dr. Phil asks), "is that working out for you?"

People will have a chance to comment on what seems to be working, what challenges they have encountered, and to tell you about other things you can do to promote their continuing success. Some things will be working out better than planned, others won't—what is important is that you are reminding them of the fact that you are interested in change and their success, and that you want to know how to make things better. The same general approach used for the predictive assessment work makes the verification assessment work.

- Be sure to get this assessment out within 30–45 days of the predictive assessment.
- The issues you should address include questions about what changes have been occurring, what observable behaviors will people start making note of, and how information has been applied; you can ask more but include these topics for sure.
- Be sure to ask what barriers to success still exist or have popped up, and be ready to take action on the information that you get from the assessment.
- Process the data as rapidly as possible (close the assessment within seven days and start doing the analysis and reporting).
- Be sure to report out the results as widely as you can—people love to know that they have been heard.

Again, although there are some sample items provided here, they are just suggestions as to what might be used. You should use your experience with your organization and your overall behavioral outcome strategies to guide your questions. It is good to keep the focus consistent between assessments. That is, ask about many of the same things here that you did during the predictive assessment.

The training has helped me to better plan my sales calls.
☐ I would not say that ☐ Maybe some, but not much ☐ True, it has ☐ It has made a big difference
The training program is helping me increase the average size of my sales commitments.
☐ I would not say that ☐ Maybe some, but not much ☐ True, it has ☐ It has made a big difference
I now use several new techniques that have made my calls more productive for both the client and for me.
☐ I would not say that ☐ Maybe some, but not much ☐ True, it has ☐ It has made a big difference

Please indicate any of the following statements that are true for you at least in part because of the training. (In other words, you may have been good at these things *already*, but if the training made you *better*, please let us know.)
- ☐ I now better understand the competition.
- ☐ I now better understand the unique advantages of my company's offerings over the competition.
- ☐ I am now better at probing for customer needs.
- ☐ I am now better at defining customer concerns.
- ☐ I am now better at overcoming price objections (presenting the value proposition).
- ☐ I engage in "feature dumping" less—I am better at aligning benefits with customer/prospect needs.

127

☐ I do more pre-call planning now than before.

☐ I have more clearly-defined call objectives than I did before.

Sales Effectiveness

☐ Actual numbers are improving (larger sales, more sales, etc.).

☐ There is less time being spent in "reselling" to existing clients.

☐ I think we will lose less business to the competition.

☐ People are feeling more comfortable in sharing information about their requirements to help me address needs.

Please tell us about anything that may present a barrier to your success. (You may remain anonymous—we just need to know what to improve.)

Final Tip: If you decide that you want to create a third phase validation assessment involving outside observers, you will want to let the respondents know on *this survey* that the next survey will include observations. You may also want to include a space on this survey for the respondents to nominate some folks who they feel would be effective observers.

Validate Success

By now, we have set our behavioral expectations, defined desired behaviors, predicted outcomes, and verified progress along with removing obstacles. It is time to see what has been observable by other people. Some organizations consider reports from "outside observers" to be somehow more believable than self-reported outcomes.

Indeed, there is a new perspective introduced when we go beyond those involved in the process for feedback. But just as eyewitness accounts of events vary, so do the impressions collected from evaluations offered up by observers. It is important to consider their perspective but seldom should the opinion of one group be held as more accurate than the opinion of another group. As the early twentieth-century poet, William Butler Yeats wrote, "The truth probably lies somewhere between . . ."

It is important to note that changes that have gotten a good start here may continue to happen as time goes on — some things that are not observable yet by others may manifest themselves. It is important to keep considering the comments and self-observations as continuing predictors. Be sure to keep updating stakeholders. The administrative steps used in the previous two assessments work essentially the same here:

- Select and advise your selected observers that they will be asked to give feedback about certain individuals.
- Make sure they know who they are observing and that the individuals know who their observers are as well.
- Let the observers see a list of behaviors that they will be looking for (if available, provide them with the assessment instrument).
- Encourage discussion between observers and participants of the process to reinforce ideas and increase awareness of behavioral objectives.
- Be sure to get this assessment out within about 75–90 days of the predictive assessment.

- The issues you should address include questions about what changes have been occurring, what observable behaviors should be noticed, and how information has been applied; you can ask more but include these topics for sure.
- Be sure to ask what barriers to success still exist or have popped up, and be ready to take action on the information that you get from the assessment.
- Process the data as rapidly as possible (close the assessment within seven days and start doing the analysis and reporting).
- Be sure to report out the results as widely as you can—people love to know that they have been heard.

Remember that the dual purpose of these assessments is to influence behavior as well as record performance. Encouraging discussion and attention on the desired behaviors will likely enhance and encourage the performance of those behaviors—that is a good thing!

The wording of items will not vary much from the previous assessment items, except the frame of reference for the observers needs to be reflected. Here are a few samples:

The training appears to have helped <the rated person> to better plan her/his sales calls.

☐ I would not say that ☐ Maybe some, but not much ☐ True, it has ☐ It has made a big difference

The training program has helped <the rated person> increase the average size of his/her sales commitments.

☐ I would not say that ☐ Maybe some, but not much ☐ True, it has ☐ It has made a big difference

<The rated person>now uses several new techniques that have made her/his calls more productive for both the client and for <the rated person>.

☐ I would not say that ☐ Maybe some, but not much ☐ True, it has ☐ It has made a big difference

It is important that the questions reflect behaviors that can be observed or deduced by watching the person being assessed. Avoid statements that call for rating subjective topics like knowledge or attitude.

Confirm Results

Remember, we are still dealing with people, not widgets—the reported behaviors and ultimate results may not match precisely as planned. It may be discovered that unintended outcomes, both positive and negative, have resulted from the learned behavior changes. In most cases, if careful planning was given to the desired behavioral changes, the anticipated results will follow. In any event, what you will find is that you have managed to achieve the desired behavioral outcomes in a clearly defensible manner, and that a lot of what you anticipated has happened.

This phase will demonstrate the success of the initiative by:

- Tying learning outcomes to behaviors to business outcomes
- Continually reinforcing behavior change by asking about it and removing obstacles to success
- Keeping stakeholders looped in so they are not wondering what happened with no data to guide them
- Creating predictions—maybe not perfect ones, but at least directional; there is some guidance toward a goal rather than a "spray and pray" approach

By employing these steps, the linkage between learning, behavioral, and business outcomes will be reinforced in the minds of all involved. Actionable information will have been provided throughout the course of the intervention. Increased engagement of the participants and stakeholders will have occurred.

In Conclusion

This cycle is iterative. Certain behaviors will have accomplished the desired goals. Other behaviors may be slightly missing the mark. With the continuing feedback loop that is provided by the OOE model, a framework for the next step is already being laid out for the next round of interventions. No one ever promised that behavioral change would be easy, but at least it is better controlled and guided than ever before. The focus of the OOE process (like all of my recommended assessments) is on the positive outcomes of the effort with a watchful eye toward what can still be changed to get better results. Now go get some plums for your pet iguana, but hurry back — the next chapter is really interesting.

Chapter 11: *Creating Questions That Get the Information You Need and Want*

I certainly hope that you have fed your iguana and shampooed your porcupine so that you are not distracted—this chapter is too fascinating to have you interrupted. It combines art, science, and street wisdom to prepare you to be your organization's "go to" person for developing surveys and assessments. You are going to like this one . . .

We will focus in on a few simple-to-understand, simple-to-implement ideas that will make survey-question design very effective. The sections include:

- The Mind's "Eye"
- Thinking Like a Human
- Engaging Your Respondent
- Designing the Survey Around the Report You Don't Have Yet

The Mind's Eye

Our brains are magnificent organs. Our brains do things that we don't even know they are doing all to make our lives easier—if we would just let them operate naturally. Unfortunately, human brain function seems to be a stumbling block for many would-be survey designers. Whether they are Mad Scientists, Guardians, or Poet Laureates, they seem uncomfortable with trusting the incredible processing power and speed of the human mind. Each, in her or his own way, struggles to corral the respondent's reactions and thereby guide the respondent to selected "acceptable" answer sets.

The Mad Scientist, if you recall, wants to strip out all emotion from responses to keep them "balanced," "objective," and "rational." The Guardian wants to control the mechanism that you use to respond so closely that you have no way to circumvent the survey/assessment process—you either comply with the instructions or very undesirable things will happen to your response set (and maybe even you). The Poet Laureate is completely convinced that your mind cannot sort through shades of meaning to get to the essence of a question and that you will react to the slightest variation in wording, potentially careening off into a ditch of misunderstanding.

Addressing the Mad Scientist

Let's talk about rational versus emotional thinking. It has been a cultural norm for many of us to treat rational decision-making as "better" than decisions based on a primarily emotional reaction, especially when the effects will be widespread or long lasting. This position has been institutionalized in the American judicial system and the court systems of many nations. In fact, whenever organizations attempt to establish a process for rendering fair, balanced, and defensible judgments (e.g., figure skating competitions, dog and cat shows, beauty pageants), significant effort is put forth to publish standards of evaluation and to allow only individuals with certain acceptable credentials or specialized training to vote on the outcomes. (I presume they do this for the purpose of, at some level, mimicking the stringent rules of order and review applied to the judiciary.)

I can't help myself. I have to ask a few questions.

- Let's talk Beagles. The American Kennel Club has a number of "standards" for quality. Take for example, the eyes:

Eyes large, set well apart – soft and hound-like – expression gentle and pleading, of a brown or hazel color. A defect list includes: eyes small, sharp and terrier-like, or prominent and protruding.[21]

If we are going to be completely "rational," from where were these standards derived? If "terrier-like" eyes are a defect, does that mean that terriers' eyes are therefore defective in an absolute sense? What objective standard defines "soft" eyes?

- Arguably one of the most famous and revered "judges" in history was King Solomon, celebrated for his wisdom. In his legendary decision to award a child to one of two petitioners, he based his decision solely on the emotional reaction of one of the parties.[22] What's up with that? A rational decision based on a third-party emotional reaction?

---

[21] These standards are an excerpt from the AKC web site referencing "Beagle Breed Standard – Hound Group," which can be found at http://www.akc.org/breeds/beagle/

[22] The popular accounting is that Solomon suggested dividing a baby in two to determine its real mother. The story is from the Old Testament of the Bible in the book of Kings. In this often-quoted passage, two prostitutes came before Solomon to resolve a quarrel about which of them was the true mother of a baby. (The other's baby died in the night and each claimed the surviving child as hers.) When Solomon suggested dividing the living child in two with a sword,

Let's look at emotions from the psycho-physiological perspective. Emotions are complex evaluative (positive or negative) reactions of the nervous system in response to external or internal stimuli (e.g., fear, sadness, anger, happiness, surprise, ambivalence, and others). Different types of emotions are associated with relatively distinct patterns of subjective (internal) experience, overt behavior (e.g., crying or laughter), motivational states (e.g., approach or avoidance), physiological arousal, learning, and activity in the nervous system.

It is widely accepted that emotions are evolutionary *adaptations*, because they enhance an organism's ability to experience and evaluate its environment and thus increase its likelihood to survive and reproduce. Loosely translated, emotional reactions are based on experience and serve as a shortcut to decision-making.

For example, let's assume you, as a child, were stung by a honey bee. Sadly, you had a violent allergic reaction to the bee sting. It is now twenty-five years later, you are walking with some friends through a wildlife preserve, and you discover you are in a field heavily populated by flowers and bees. The disruption caused by you and your friends walking through the field has disturbed the bees and they appear to be swarming. You have an emotional reaction to the stimulus, become frightened, and scamper away from the field as fast as you can, with the sounds of laughter and shouts of "wussy boy!" from your friends ringing in your ears. The good news is that you avoid any further direct unpleasantness from the insects—the bad

---

the true mother was revealed to him because she was willing to give up her child to the lying woman rather than have the child killed. Solomon then declared that the woman who showed compassion was the true mother and handed the child to her.

Addressing the Guardian

We all want to feel that our surveys and assessments are as free as possible from malicious tampering, and there will always be an element who likes to toy with processes just for the sake of seeing what will happen. I doubt there are many people who are passionate enough about any survey or assessment (with the exception of qualifying or certifying examinations or psychological profiling instruments) that they would want to deliberately circumvent their processes, except for pure entertainment value to see if they can't "outsmart" the survey or get it to react in some odd way. Little do they realize that most survey administrations *automatically* produce very odd results due to inept design or administration; they would be hard-pressed to make them much sillier.

"You will NOT mark outside the bubbles!
You WILL erase any stray marks!"

Therefore, I will leave this section quite brief. A sur·
about a training class or even a multi-rater assessme
organizational leadership is not likely to generate e
grass-roots passion to cause people to spend any ·

1

fixing the outcomes. There is of course the inevitable misinterpretation of items, the failure to follow basic instructions, and the confusion over how to complete the forms. Assuming that you have a fairly standard, intuitive format with simple to read and follow instructions for completion, the percentage of completion errors will be minimal. Making heroic efforts to avoid multiple responses by a single person, or identity spoofing of a name by someone else, or fears of revealing the contents of questions among potential respondents is likely to make the administration more difficult and cumbersome. We want to avoid difficult and cumbersome. We are largely past the era of using #2 pencils and darkening only inside the lines (a mark of real social evolution, in my opinion).

In my years of survey design and administration, the bigger challenge is in getting high response rates, not in preventing overly zealous people from taking the assessments too frequently or attempting to influence the results. I will welcome the day when we write such engaging instruments that our biggest problem is people caring about the outcomes too much.

Addressing the Poet Laureate

This is an interesting aspect to survey design. On one hand, you want to be sure that you will get all the information you need, that the question was properly understood by the respondent, and that the question is fully answerable. On the other hand, you want to make sure that the respondents are sufficiently engaged by the question items that they will not feel so much like the subjects of some sort of scientific inquiry. Too much formal language makes them feel like they are being examined under a microscope, and that in turn makes them less natural in their responses. It is my position that as long as the question is fully answerable, the rest of the item design can err on the side of being too conversational.

To illustrate "fully answerable," here are some examples of items that do NOT qualify:

- Do you drive to work or carry a sack lunch?
  ☐ I drive ☐ I bring my lunch to work
  (This one is easy — a person could do neither or both of these things — "or" is an inappropriate conjunction to use here. It needs to be broken into two separate question items.)
- Did you find the instructor entertaining and informative? ☐ Yes ☐No
  (Now it gets just a bit trickier — this is called a "double-barreled" question; it can be interpreted several ways. If the instructor was BOTH entertaining and informative or NEITHER entertaining nor informative, we will probably get a valid response. But what if the instructor was entertaining but offered nothing new to the respondent in terms of learning? What if the instructor dropped lots of pearls of wisdom but was otherwise kind of a boring presenter? What will the respondent do then — opt for the "NO" answer because both conditions were not met? Opt for the "YES" answer because at least one condition was met? Not respond because either answer feels wrong? It is very hard to say — different people react in different ways to this condition. The solution is to make this into two separate questions.)

- Please indicate your favorite household pet from the list below:
  ☐ Dog ☐ Cat ☐ Parakeet ☐ Goldfish
  (This is another common error in question design. What if your favorite pet is a canary, porcupine, bat, or seahorse? What if you don't like pets at all? The designer failed to allow for all the possible options, which in turn may get invalid results. At a minimum, there should be the options of "Other type of pet" and "No pet at all" to capture most expected responses.)
- Do you favor increased funding for research and use of the tyrosine kinase inhibitors imatinib and gefitinib *even if* it is at the expense of research and development of the anti-HER2/neu antibody trastuzumab (Herceptin) and anti-CD20 antibody rituximab? ☐ Yes ☐ No
  (As important a scientific and ethical question as this may be, it is inappropriate for most audiences. Be sure that your question items are fully answerable based on the presumed background of your respondents.)

In summary then, if question items are understandable by your audience, allow for the full range of possible responses,[25] and are not "double-barreled," the rest of the

---

[25] There is such a thing as a "forced choice" format that does not allow for a neutral or non-committal answer, which is often used in assessments designed to classify the respondent by psychological type (construct) or simply to prevent too many non-directional answers. These do have their place if the reason for them is fully supportable. Generally, even forced choice responses allow for skip-

process of question item design becomes fairly straight-forward, as you will see.

There is a great deal of concern among new survey and test designers about using the "proper" wording for items. There is a widespread belief that precision wording is critical to a respondent's understanding of what is being asked. In larger organizations, there is a great deal of time spent by internal staff people who want to "word-smith" survey and assessment item to make sure they work as intended. Ultimately, after numerous reviews and revisions, my clients are finally satisfied with the wording of the assessment, the survey goes out, and *viola!* The instrument gets the quality of information hoped for. It seems to happen every time. Is it because I only work with incredibly intelligent clients with a real mastery of language? Well, yes, I do, but that is not the reason. Although my clients are all brilliant, the reason that the surveys and assessments seem always to work is more basic. Let me explain.

Look at the four items below. Do you think the reactions would vary significantly based on which query item (below) was used?

- The class met my expectations. ☐True ☐False
- The class accomplished the goals I had in mind. ☐ True ☐ False
- The class objectives as I understood them were achieved. ☐True ☐ False

---

ping the questions or a "cannot say/decline to answer response," however.

- I got what I expected from the class. ☐True☐False

Generally Unacknowledged Measurement Principle #7:
It doesn't make much difference how you word your items if they are structurally sound and have appropriate response mechanisms associated with them.

That's right. The human mind kicks in and straightens out most anything that is not quite right so the intention of the question is generally understood correctly. Don't believe me? Okay, read this passage below:

I cdnuolt blveiee taht I cluod aulaclty uesdnatnrd waht I was rdanieg. The phaonmneal pweor of the hmuan mnid. Aoccdrnig to rscheearch at Cmabrigde Uinervtisy, it deosn't mttaer in waht oredr the ltteers in a wrod are, the olny iprmoatnt tihng is taht the frist and lsat ltteer be in the rghit pclae. The rset can be a taotl mses and you can sitll raed it wouthit a porbelm. Tihs is bcuseae the huamn mnid deos not raed ervey lteter by istlef, but the wrod as a wlohe. Amzanig, huh?[26]

I will be the first to admit that it is probably better not to jumble your letters up inside words when creating a survey. However, I will also stand by my position that survey items intended for a general audience can be well

---

[26] This is taken from a widely circulated email novelty that has roots going back to 2003 or even earlier. It has been slightly modified and attribution incorrectly given to researchers at the University of Cambridge, who take some issue with the theory espoused in the text. If you are into jumbling up English words (perhaps for your next survey), you can use a neat little tool you can find on the web: http://www.stevesachs.com/jumbler.cgi

communicated by using the vernacular. I personally believe that for most general audiences, it is actually superior to a formal literary writing style for surveys.

Thinking Like a Human

There is a characteristic of surveys that seldom seems to come up in design sessions or even professional conferences. Simply put, a survey or questionnaire is a somewhat invasive tool. People will respond honestly to questions through written and online surveys that might create hesitation or outright embarrassment if asked face-to-face. There is a certain sense of anonymity provided by surveys that does not exist in normal conversation. By wording things in non-formal language, we more closely reflect the way that people think private thoughts to themselves. This, I believe, actually enhances the sense of positive intimacy that is required to get the most honest (aka least socially compliant) responses.

Certainly formal language, especially the English language, can be used with tremendous precision if words are chosen with great care. The effort to create extraordinary precision is misplaced in most opinion and reaction surveys because we don't think in precision terms when we have a reaction. We tend toward a more holistic response.

For example, consider your reaction to any film that you recently viewed. Let's say you saw the movie at a "sneak preview" event and that the movie was just out in limited release. Now let's say someone wanted to get your reaction (and the reaction of a few thousand others) to the experience in order to decide whether to spend the money to get wide distribution of the movie, and to create after-market products. The basic questions the investor would need to have answered would include the following:

- Did you enjoy the movie?
- Will you tell your friends to go see it?
- Will you pay to see it again?
- Would you buy a copy of it for personal viewing at home?
- Were you so impressed by any of the characters that you are inclined to want to dress or act like them (even a little)?
- Would you like to have a memento of the movie for yourself or to give as a gift?

We all know that your answers to these questions are heavily influenced by other factors, which may or may not have been associated with the movie-going experience. These factors could include:

- Who you went with and whether that made the experience better or worse
- If you were able to get "into" the film or were distracted by others in the theater
- How you felt emotionally and physically while you were there
- What you did immediately before and after the movie
- Where you sat and how comfortable the seating was
- The way the theater staff treated you

In fact, there could be hundreds of other factors that affected your overall experience. But again, the human mind thinks holistically, and questions drilling down to the secondary factors are both tiring to the person being asked and irrelevant to the information the investor/stakeholder needs.

The reason for mentioning all this is that when you set out to design a survey, do so in as holistic a fashion as you can. The additional information you ask for might only serve to reduce your response rate, reduce the quality of responses you get overall (due to mental fatigue from your respondents), and provide your stakeholders with irrelevant and/or distracting information.

> When you set out to design a survey, do so in as holistic a fashion as you can.

Going back to our film preview example, it is fair to assume that only the larger, more holistic impressions of the movie are what will be remembered by the viewers for any real length of time. Think about it for yourself: do you remember with any degree of specificity exactly where you sat, what the ticket-taker looked like, who sat near you, or why you liked a movie that you saw over a month ago?

Engaging Your Respondent

I have said it before, and I will say it again: people are doing you a favor by responding to your survey and assessment questions. There is a big chance that they will lose interest in helping you out by sharing their impressions and opinions if they start to see a diminished payoff to themselves. Make every effort to make them feel good about taking and completing your question set. How can we do that?

Keep the Number of Questions as Small as Possible

There is little that will turn off a potential respondent as much as thinking that the question and answer cycle will go on for too long. It makes no difference whether the potential respondent has anything whatsoever to do for the next fifteen to twenty minutes. If she or he thinks that a dispro-

"Before you leave, please fill out this questionnaire."

portionate amount of time relative to the topic will be required, the likelihood of participation is greatly reduced.

Use Flattery

President James Monroe once said, "A little flattery will support a man through great fatigue." A more apt quote would be hard to find regarding asking people to fill out questionnaires. Most people find them tiring and monotonous. Therefore, feel free to gush a bit by telling them just how important their opinions are and how desperately you need their insights. Once inside the survey, periodically give some form of positive reinforcement of their good behavior. It might be one of those completion thermometers that shows them just how far they have progressed. Perhaps you could enter a comment at the end of each page, thanking them for their continued participation. And of course, thank them at the end of the survey. Best of all, show them your flattery was grounded in sincerity by communicating to them after the survey is over what you did with the information or what other people besides them had to say. That makes the next request for participation a bit simpler because they see that you listened to them the last time.

Making the Query Items Interesting

To the greatest extent possible, keep the query items themselves conversational and brief, but if need be, provide an introductory statement to the question to get their attention. The introduction can be of reasonable length if it serves the purpose of stimulating an opinion. For example, consider the difference between these two item sets:

Poor Form —

"I believe that painting a bat's toenails should only be done by a professional manicurist."

☐ Yes ☐ No

In the above example, people may not be fully engaged in the issue at hand—they may have never even considered the proposition before, rendering their opinions casual at best.

Interesting Form (using an introduction) —

There are people who consider the sport/fad of capturing a bat for the sole purpose of applying nail polish to it to be time-consuming, risky, and downright silly with no real benefit to anyone. Those who support the activity are divided on the issue of who should be involved. We need your reaction to the following item (please assume that a bat is in an appropriate setting to have nail polish applied).

I believe that painting a bat's toenails should only be done by a professional manicurist."

☐ Yes ☐ No

In this example, regardless of how people feel about painting bats' toenails, they feel somehow valued for their opinion. They also will have a heightened sense of responsibility for their answer. In other words, they are more engaged; what was a question of no relevance is now a question about which they may feel some responsibility or passion.

There are other features of a survey design that can be introduced to make the experience more engaging, but they are more closely related to the response mechanisms than the query items themselves and are therefore postponed until the next chapter. But to engage, remember these three principles:
1. Keep the instrument as brief as practical.
2. Use flattery and encouragement early and often.
3. Make the queries as interesting as possible — the respondents need to care about their answers.

Designing Your Survey Around the Report You Don't Have Yet

We will close this chapter with some design suggestions. It is really darn easy to get so caught up in the process that we lose sight of the objective, which is to get the stakeholders information that they can use. This process is actually two-fold:
*   Identifying the questions to be answered
*   Deciding on the form that will be best received

Identifying the Questions to be Answered

I know this sounds very basic and simplistic, but so do the rules of chess. I mean, what is the big deal? Six different pieces — you want to capture the king piece; each of the pieces has a strict movement pattern on the board. How hard can that be, right? Same thing with survey design. Often the stakeholders only have a vague idea of what they want to know. They think they know what they want to know but they don't. They are too close to the issue or they are too worried about what the survey instrument will look like.

The approach to find out what is needed is at least straightforward. Ask what the stakeholders hope to *do* with the information when they get it, then walk back from that point. A convenient example is the movie example from a section or two back, which is reproduced here:

The stakeholder/investor needs to decide whether to spend the money to get wide distribution of the movie, and to create after-market products.

By walking backwards from this point, we can eliminate a lot of questions about the theaters, the time people went, what else they did before and after, and any number of demographic questions. The list of things that the stakeholders don't need to know is virtually endless.

What they do need to know is whether there will be enough positive "buzz" about the movie to get more people willing to pay to see it, how many will pay to see it a second or more times, whether there is a market for CDs, and what ancillary products could be licensed and sold. It is probably wise to run some demographic analysis to see if there are population segments that are more inclined to support the venture, but let's assume that part will be handled by the marketing department. All you want to know are the answers to the primary questions, which are shown here. The basic questions the investor would need to have answered would include the following:

- Did you enjoy the movie?
- Will you tell your friends to go see it?
- Will you pay to see it again?
- Would you buy a copy of it for personal viewing at home?
- Were you so impressed by any of the characters that you are inclined to want to dress or act like them (even a little)?
- Would you like to have a memento of the movie for yourself or to give as a gift?

That is your framework. From there, one or two direct, well-worded, engaging questions will collect the information.[27]

Deciding On the Form That Will Be Best Received

This is a matter of personal preference on the part of your stakeholders. You need to know how sophisticated they are as consumers of survey information. Are they able to read and interpret charts, graphs, and tables? Do they prefer a narrative report? How will they want the information presented? These delivery questions will help frame the way the questions are worded specifically and what the response mechanisms should look like. Below is a table that explains the strengths of different types of graphs:

---

[27] Of course, there are elements of proper survey sampling that need to be considered, but for our purposes here, let's assume the stakeholders have an idea of who to survey and how to get the surveys to the target population. This chapter is long enough as it is.

Type	Strengths
Bar Chart	Easy to compare multiple values (such as percent of various age groups that would see the film a second time)
Line Chart	Good for showing changes over time (like the increase in ticket sales over a six week period or as more theaters pick up the film)
Pie Chart	To show what grouping contributed to the total of something (like the percentage of men vs. women who liked the movie or the percentage of people from the Northeast, Southeast, Southwest, and Northwest who liked the movie)
Scatter Chart	To compare pairs of values (like chronological age of viewers and the overall rating of the film given)
Histo-gram	To classify some measure by categories (like specific age groupings and the percent of people who would buy the CD of the movie or the sound track)

Here are what the charts look like for reference:

Bar Chart

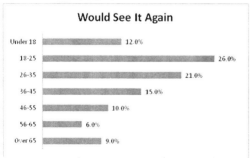

Line Chart

Pie Chart

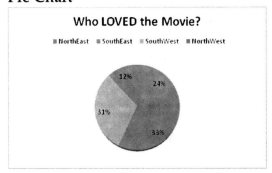

Scatter Chart

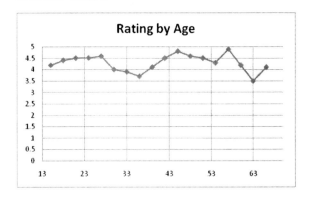

Histogram[28]

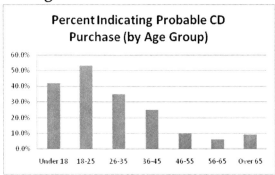

These data display samples represent various types of collected data. The actual data that gets collected is in turn dictated by the response mechanism, which goes along with the query items. For example, a "yes/no" question would produce numbers easily displayed in the bar chart. An interval scaling system, which produced values that could be anywhere between one and five, for example, might be best displayed on the scatter chart, and so forth. We will cover that business later. The important thing is to design your questions to get both the important information and the information in a form that can be understood.

Long chapter. Go give your porcupine some love. He probably wonders what you have been up to.

---

[28] Technically, this is columnar chart and not a histogram. The edges of a histogram actually touch each other because the groupings are very precise. A histogram can be produced by higher-end statistical software packages.

Chapter 12: *Using Scaling Systems That Make Sense*

C an I get a show of hands of everyone who has done any of the following?

1. Drank a liquid by placing the lips on the *upper* edge of the glass as opposed to the traditional bottom edge
2. Used a tennis racquet to drain water off of pasta
3. Attempted to drive a railroad spike into a wall using a crystal vase so that you would have a hook to hang a small picture

If so, how did it work for you?

In example #1, although the right tools (cup and mouth) are employed, they are employed in a less-than-optimally-effective way. In example #2, we are attempting to do things the right way but using a tool that was designed primarily for something else. In the third example, we have reasonable intentions but are using inappropriate tools and will get a less-than-optimal result. More often than you might think, surveys and assessments suffer from similar challenges; they are designed with mismatched items and scaling systems, but unlike the examples above, the less-than-optimal results of assessments may not be discovered, as we see in the next section.

"My Instructor Was Terribly Excellent": A True Story[29]

The psychology department of a major university system typically conducted end-of-course student evaluation surveys as a regular part of their program. For twenty-four years, it had used the same forms with the same scaling system to evaluate courses. The scaling system was a variation of the five-point Likert scale and used the response anchors, "excellent," "very good," "good," "poor," and "terrible." During the twenty-fifth year of administration of the form, some changes were made that included the more traditional "strongly disagree-to-strongly agree" format with which we are all familiar. A year or two after the conversion to the new scaling system, the psychology department chair requested that the survey have a couple of new query items added to it. The form was still to have used the new "strongly disagree–to–strongly agree" format.

During the revision of the instrument, the clerk creating the form inadvertently entered the old anchors of "excellent–to–terrible" against all the new query items. The resulting response items included statements like, "I always come to class" with "excellent–to–terrible" as response choices.

The survey was administered to twenty-seven classes representing hundreds of students. Several outcomes were discovered:

---

[29] The following summary is taken from a research article. For those interested, here is the citation: R. Sommer, "Literal Versus Metaphorical Interpretations of Scale Terms: A Serendipitous Natural Experiment," *Educational and Psychological Measurement* 51(1991): 1009-1012.

- The error was not reported by any of the instructors.
- The error was not reported by any of the respondents (the students).
- The results, when compared to earlier surveys, did not differ in any significant way; the ratings earned were virtually identical using the nonsensical form as had been earned during previous years!

So what went upside-down in this case? A few things:

- The main "players" involved (i.e., the instructors and students) had no particular interest in what was being asked; class was over—everybody wanted to go home.
- There was likely nothing engaging about the instrument to hold anyone's attention.
- There was apparently not much that was done with the information to cause the people directly involved with the ratings to care about outcomes.
- Most of the items were using an inappropriate scale in the first place, which over time contributed to the indifference.

Before we leave this particular example, let's examine the item that was used in the research article: "I always come to class."

The original author was suggesting the response options of "excellent–to–terrible" were silly. I agree. But I have to question just how much better the choices would have been had they used the standard "strongly agree" to "strongly disagree" options as intended. In my corner of the world, if I am going to confirm if someone *always* comes to class, I suspect that I might ask, "Do you *always* come to class?" and be looking for a "yes" or "no" answer. If I wanted to get a read on the frequency of class attendance, I might ask for the percent of time one comes to class or what the ratio of absences to class sessions the respondent had. I seriously doubt that I would treat the issue as a response calling for an *opinion*, however.

The use of Likert scaling when other response mechanisms are more appropriate is probably the most common error in survey scale design. Incidentally, this would probably be the Type #2 error (tennis racquet to drain pasta). To help keep these ideas in order I am offering up some basic rules. Here is the first one:

Scaling Rule #1
If you are attempting to determine if something IS or IS NOT a true condition, allow for a binary response.[30]

Speaking of Binary Response Formats . . . We Were, Weren't We?

The only caution that I would offer when asking a binary response question is to be fairly certain that the respondent can reasonably be expected to know the

---

[30] A binary response is "yes/no," "true/false," "black/white," etc.

answer. People will have a tendency to offer a response, even if they are not sure if they are correct or fully believe what they are telling you. In other words, binary response formats work very well if asking someone about their own personal experiences, behaviors, or opinions about things they really have thought about. For example, if you ask, "Did you ever have chicken pox?" people should be able to answer you with confidence and accuracy either "yes" or "no." But if you ask, "Would you like to see someone like Millard Fillmore in the Oval Office next year?" there is no telling whether the answers you get would really reflect the respondents' attitudes unless they were well-schooled on the Fillmore presidency and Mr. Fillmore's policies. Be sure to know the frame of reference of your audience.

A Brief Look at Likert Scaling—And Things I Bet You Didn't Know

Now let's get back to the Likert Scale and its many variations. Remember, when Rensis Likert first developed his namesake scale during the first half of the twentieth-century, he was attempting to use it to measure social attitudes. The statements to which people were to react were generally simple declarative statements about broad issues. For example, a person might be asked to indicate her or his level of (dis)agreement with a series of statements about the overall performance of the Federal government. For example:

Please indicate how much you agree or disagree with each of these statements:

Question	Neither	Agree Strongly	Agree Somewhat	Agree Strongly	Disagree
The president is doing a good job.	1	2	3	4	5
The Congress is doing a good job.	1	2	3	4	5
The Judicial Branch is doing a good job.	1	2	3	4	5

If you want to elicit some serious opinions about major issues, it is hard to beat the Likert Scaling System. It was designed for just that purpose. But if you are planning on using this system, it is going to be to your advantage to know how to use it correctly.

The Likert Scaling System was intended to be used with *several* Likert statements, which are grouped together.[31] In the example above, we are asking for attitudes about the Federal government, and in reality, there would probably be a few more item statements that needed to be added to the list to make sure we had enough response data for purposes of calculation. Why, you ask? Simple. In this example, we are really measuring somebody's view of the performance of the Federal government as a *whole*, not just an opinion about the different *branches*

---

[31] Remember, the Likert Scaling *System* consists of Likert **statement** *items* (e.g., "The President is doing a good job") and the Likert **response scale** (e.g., 1, 2, 3, 4, and 5). The *items* and the *scale* combine to make one system.

of the government.32 So we might need to add some items about the IRS or Homeland Security or the other cabinet departments that operate under the President's direction. See, somebody might like the President and think that the way Congress and the Judiciary perform is fine overall. At the same time however, they might think that the IRS, departments of commerce, Treasury, and Homeland Security were just terribly mishandled operations. The more things you check on when using the Likert scaling system, the better off you will be in drawing conclusions about what people are telling you about the topic you chose. By increasing the number of items you ask about, the less chance you have of making the Type #1 error of using the right tools in the wrong way.

Scaling Rule #2

A Likert Scale can be used for collecting a "grouping" of opinions about a general topic. It is not good to use that type of scale if you are eliciting an opinion about a single topic.

Some Facts About Numbers That We Really Need to Cover

There is a fair chance that you have always thought of numbers as just numbers. That is not really all there is to it. Numbers are not really "things." **Numbers are ideas or concepts of amounts of something.** You might look at the symbol "7" and say to me, "What are you talking about?

---

32 Don't get confused. We *could* have just asked about the different branches and had several questions about branch operations. But in this example, we were taking a broader look than just the branches; the items need to address the totality of what we are learning about.

That is the number "7." Most anybody over the age of four knows it is 7 and that is all there is to it." Wouldn't it be nice if life was that straightforward and understandable? The problem is that as soon as "7" appeared on my computer screen (and later in the pages of this book) it no longer was the *number* "7." It became the *numeral* "7" in much the same way that I can type the name, "Mercedes Benz 500 SEL" but I can't drive the words I just wrote. Words that are written or spoken are not really the things themselves, but only verbal *representations* of those things. That is why when we write something like, "Here is how you spell the word, 'porcupine': P-O-R-C-U-P-I-N-E," we put the word that is being talked about in quotation marks. We want to show that the subject of our conversation is literally the word or words we are discussing.

Now we have to dive just a little bit deeper before we come up for air. When we write out numerals that represent numbers, we are talking about numbers that in turn represent values that people have assigned to them. We have to be very careful what we do with the values that are represented. Sometimes the numbers we are talking about represent some sort of a count of something. That would be when we say, "I spent twenty minutes standing in line." That means that if we all understand the concept of a minute, we can mentally multiply that period of time by twenty in our minds and get an idea of how much time was spent waiting in line. When you use the number twenty this way, mathematicians would say you were using a *rational number*. (More about that later.)

But let's say you filled out a form that called for a response of "male" or "female" and for purposes of shorthand, the response value of "male" was assigned the numeral "1" and "female" was assigned the value of "2." In this case, the value of "2" could just as easily been assigned to the response "male" and the value of "1" assigned to the response "female." There is no requirement that either number be associated with either gender response. When numbers are arbitrarily assigned in this way, the numbers themselves are called **nominal numbers**. They are just used for shorthand purposes, but you can't really do much with them except to count how many of each response there were, like 293 people responded "1" (male) and 312 people responded "2" (female). It would not make any sense to average the numerals used and to expect to make any sense out of them. If you did, the average would be ((293 X 1) + (312 X 2)) ÷ 605 = 1.516. Nobody who filled out the form was a "1.516." What would that mean anyway?—that the "average" respondent was an effeminate male or a masculine female?

You see how silly it is to do a lot of mathematical calculations on nominal numbers. That is an example of the Type #3 error of having good intentions but using inappropriate tools, getting you a much less-than-optimal result. Now let's take the kind of numbers you get when you complete a Likert Scale (or other scales that call for degrees of opinion like "strongly agree," "agree," "neutral," "disagree," or "strongly disagree"). These numbers can be used for more than just shorthand labels, but they are not good enough to be used like the rational numbers. When numbers are used to show where a response falls along some *continuum* or line like:

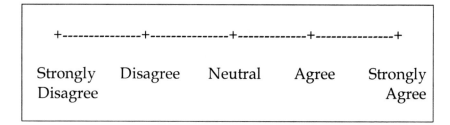

```
+---------------+---------------+-------------+---------------+

Strongly      Disagree      Neutral      Agree      Strongly
Disagree                                               Agree
```

those numbers are referred to as **ordinal numbers.** That is because they are used to show the order or ranking of choices. If we assigned the numeral "1" to "strongly disagree," "2" to "disagree," and so on, we could see where someone ranked or ordered their responses. What we cannot say is that the emotional "distance" (or strength of the opinions) is equally spaced between each of the responses.

Here is an example to illustrate. (For those of you who have pet porcupines, this will sound familiar.) It is a bright, sunny day, and you decide that it is time to shampoo your porcupine. Because you know how fidgety he can be, you enlist the help of one of your neighbors. As so often happens, stray quills find their way into both your hands and your neighbor's hands. Being a veteran of this process, you comment to your neighbor, Heather, "Boy those quills sure do irritate."

Heather responds, "Irritate? IRRITATE?!? Are you nuts? They hurt like the devil! Look at me! I am going to have to go to the ER, you idiot!"

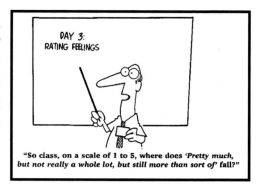

DAY 3:
RATING FEELINGS

"So class, on a scale of 1 to 5, where does 'Pretty much, but not really a whole lot, but still more than sort of' fall?"

166

Now if each of you were to fill out a questionnaire about how you felt responding to the statement, "Being stuck with porcupine quills hurts significantly," you might respond "neutral" or "agree."

Probably Heather would respond with a rating of "strongly agree." There is no question that Heather feels that the quill stings hurt her more than she thinks they hurt you. The big question is, how much more do they hurt *her* than *you*? Because she is new to porcupine shampooing and because she does not have the same bond you may have with your pet, her reaction is certainly more severe and her skin may in fact be more tender. (But we don't know that for sure. Maybe she is just more excitable.) Regardless, we have no way of knowing exactly in common terms the exact difference of opinion. We know there is a difference of opinion for sure. The amount is still unknown—the ranking is clear. Translated into arithmetic terms, that means that we still cannot average the rankings to come up with an "average" sensitivity to porcupine quills. This response mechanism is too subjective. That, by the way, is why Dr. Likert did not bother creating equal differences between the response points on his scale. To do so is kind of silly, because people have different ideas of how much difference there is between strongly agreeing and simply agreeing. Dr. Likert just said "To heck with it—we'll treat the data as ordinal only."[33] Once again, "ordinal" means the order of something only—not the spacing between the things in question.

---

[33] For the literal readers among us, I have no idea if Dr. Likert really said, "To heck with it-- we'll treat the data as ordinal only." I am just speculating on that part. One way or another he did communicate that idea when writing about his scaling system, though.

Scaling Rule #3

Scaling systems that use Likert-like scale values should NEVER be averaged together. They are best counted and presented in a chart or table.

Hang in there. We are almost done. I mentioned earlier that there were times when number values could be treated as rational numbers. Treating numbers as rational numbers is — dare I say it? — rational when you are administering some sort of quiz or test and assigning a score based on the number of correct answers. That is because the numbers earned on the test have an absolute meaning and equally separated values. 100 percent means that somebody got everything right; 50 percent means they got half right; the person who got 75 percent did three-quarters as well as the person who got the 100 percent, and so on. The scores can be averaged to see how people did overall. You can do just about any kind of mathematical manipulation that you want to with the data and it can tell a "story" of sorts. Just remember that if you are hoping to perform a bunch of mathematical operations on numeric results, you want to make sure that the data can handle it. One last thing — there is a type of numeric data that is called *interval data.* It is pretty much like rational data in that you can do all that fun averaging and other statistical magic to it. What is the difference between rational data and interval data? Not much. Both have equally separated values, like points on a thermometer or mile markers on a highway. If you really, really want to learn more than that, let me suggest you pick up a basic statistics text and read up on the subject. (I have readers to entertain and inform here — I can't torture them any further with this stuff.) As far as surveys and assessments go, figure that interval and rational data are pretty much alike. When you can get that type of data, it is a good thing—but not that easy to do in most cases. In the next chapter, I will show you one way you can get that quality of information. For now, let's just go on with the more traditional methods.

Scaling Rule #4

If you want to be able to compute averages, standard deviations, and other more sophisticated analyses, you have to use rational or interval data. Only a few scaling systems can provide that type of data, though—be careful!

Getting Back to Other Scaling Concepts . . . Finally

A scaling system that has enjoyed increasing popularity along with increasing use of online survey methods is the "Discrete Visual Analog Scale." Don't be frightened. It is just a complicated sounding name for a simple type of scale. You have probably seen something like this:

Just how terrific is this book, really?
Not very good O O O O O O O Totally awesome, man!

This is an effective way of allowing respondents to react to a question or statement without having to select from a predefined set of responses, and allows for a more natural way of expressing an opinion. In my opinion, it is more accurate in terms of capturing respondent reactions than the traditional Likert scaling system and starts to move us into the range of equally separated response val-

169

ues. It is easy to complete, and numeric values can be assigned to the "radio buttons" in such a way that the respondents can't see the values being assigned. This lessens their tendency to assign an "acceptable rating" instead of how they really feel. Nevertheless, this data should still not be treated as interval data because the choices are still not guaranteed to be equally spaced.

Let's move away from number-based systems now. A common response mechanism is the checkbox or drop-down list. With either of these methods, the respondent is given a pre-written selection of responses. The person completing the survey is allowed sometimes to choose only one and is sometimes permitted to choose "all that apply" or something in between.

This method is excellent for corralling responses that might otherwise be too varied to compare if a simple "fill in the blank" approach was used. The method is straight-forward and quite useful—provided that the survey designer has considered most or all of the responses possible and of interest. Let me steal a concept from the last chapter for illustration:

Please indicate the types of critters you have had as pets since childhood (check all that apply):

☐ Dog ☐ Cat ☐ Goldfish ☐ Canary
☐ Parakeet ☐ Bat ☐ Aardvark ☐ Horse
☐ Iguana ☐ Pig ☐ Snake ☐ Porcupine
☐ Cow or Bull ☐ Unicorn ☐ Flying or Tree Squirrel
☐ Other (please describe below) ☐ None

This type of response mechanism is very effective for identifying the percentages of common response sets. Values are easy to calculate and reporting is simple. It is critical to include the "other" and "none" response values to ensure that you have not unintentionally distorted the data. If you have created a comprehensive list, it is unlikely that the "Other" response will represent a particularly significant proportion of responses, and can therefore be itemized or grouped without explanation as appropriate.

Scaling Rule #5

For most scaling approaches, consider carefully including "escape" responses such as "Other," "None," "Does not apply," "I don't know," "I choose not to respond," etc. to prevent unintentional distortion of data.

The last common method of collecting data is the "fill in the blank" or "open-ended response" mechanism. This is not really a scaling method *per se*, but under certain circumstances can provide a richness of information that is hard to get any other way. The big advantage is that the respondents can put in their own words the comments that really capture their ideas and/or offer explanations for other responses that were given using other items and scales. The big disadvantage is that it is labor intensive to summarize a large volume of responses. This type of data collection is not really quantitative at all unless you are able to group or classify and then tally the responses for your stakeholders to use. For example, you might ask what someone will best remember or apply from a training program. If you got responses from people like:

- "I can identify ordinal numbers from interval numbers now,"
- "I know the difference between rational and nominal data,"
- "I won't average ordinal data anymore,"
- "I know the different types of numbers (ordinal, rational, etc.),"

...then you might be able to summarize that four people indicated an increased awareness of data types or that the discussion of the different uses of various types of data appeared to be understood by at least a segment of the population that got training. Of course, you could simply copy the responses verbatim into a report and allow the reader to draw her or his own conclusions as well.

Scaling Rule #6
No matter how good a system you have for collecting data, there is some advantage to picking up some qualitative information along the way. It is cumbersome to work with, but usually adds clarity and depth to your analysis.

In Conclusion...
This chapter is not an exhaustive treatment of all there is to know about scaling. It may have been *exhausting* but not *exhaustive*. Perhaps you picked up a few techniques about matching scaling with questions. If so, terrific. If you were able to come away with the understanding that most reports that confidently provide averages and standard deviations of results collected from surveys and assessments are seriously flawed, then it was time well spent—you have made a major jump ahead of most of your peers. If you have developed a healthy respect for

the risks associated with asking your neighbors to help you groom your pet porcupine, all the better. Next chapter: the mother of all scaling systems—the Item Response Graphic System. See you there!

Chapter 13: *Measuring in a New, Different, and Better Way*

There are a few critical factors that make the difference between collecting information that is actionable and ending up with information that is, well, marginal at best. The factors are:

- Selecting a *representative* sample from your population of interest
- Achieving a response rate sufficient to be confident that the opinions expressed represent the population you are interested in hearing from
- Causing the respondents to be engaged enough to give you a thoughtful set of answers
- Ensuring that the respondents accurately respond with what they truly think or feel
- Having data of sufficient quality that you can slice and dice in ways that give you significant information without loss of data integrity

I know that these points sound kind of technical and boring. They are important concepts, nevertheless, and for the person who is serious about getting the best possible information upon which to base decisions, it is important to understand how to reach these goals. If it helps you to remain focused, visualize yourself not reading a book but sitting in a lecture hall.

> You are reading this book for enjoyment more than edification, much like the White House Chief of Staff is doing.

The speaker is not me, but a very engaging and articulate gecko with a Cockney accent . . . (Wait. Somebody else already did that. Substitute the critter of your choice and give it a subtle Italian accent. I don't want your mind to be in violation of any copyright provisions.) Okay, let's proceed.

Selecting a Representative Sample

There are tons of textbooks available that will go into painstaking detail about how to select a random sample, or a stratified random sample, or a cluster sample, or a stratified cluster sample, or just about any kind of sample you can imagine. The good news is that I am not going to go into detail about this because for most practical applications inside organizations, doing this type of rigorous preparation is akin to bringing a gun to a knife fight. First, there probably aren't all that many people in your organization who you need to survey, of whom you would have to take just a sample. You could simply go out to the entire population of interest and encourage them all to respond.

Sampling is really good if you are responsible for the U.S. Census and responsible for keeping costs down, or are conducting exit polls for a statewide or national election where you are delivering results as fast as you can. I am going out on a limb here once again and assuming that if you make your living doing those things, you are reading this book for enjoyment more than edification, much like the White House Chief of Staff is doing. And I will further assume you don't want to ruin a good read with a lot of statistical theory.

In a nutshell, scratch this first requirement. Just do your darndest to get everybody to respond to your survey and your sample will probably be fairly representative (if you have a decent response rate). Speaking of response rates, let's go to that section.

Determining a Good Response Rate

Before I delve into the methods recommended to get a good response rate, let me give you an idea of what a good response rate is. There are three basic considerations:

- The size of the population you are measuring
- What margin of error you can live with
- How specific you want to be about what people are telling you (based on their survey responses)

The size of the population makes a big difference in how many returned surveys you need. It is not a straight-line sort of calculation, like always achieving a response rate of 25 percent, or 80 percent, or something. The reason is simple. If a person gives you an opinion about something, then another person gives you an opinion, and another, and another, you will start to see a pattern developing. After a while, you will be seeing opinions that are quite similar. If you have enough people giving you their opinions, you will eventually hear about all the opinions there are to hear. Once that starts happening, all that is left for you to figure out is what the most common opinions are—what percentage has what opinion. That is how those exit polls that are reported on the election news coverage are figured out. There are only so many candidates or issues that are being voted on, and once you start seeing a pattern, there is really not too much need to keep asking people how they voted. You can usually predict the outcome with just feedback from a small percentage of voters. It isn't perfect, but usually the exit polls pretty much tell the tale before you have to pack it in and go to bed.

Reasonably enough, if there is a great number of people giving opinions, you have to hear from a larger absolute number than if there are only a few people just because it takes more information gathering to see what the proportional pattern is. But interestingly enough, the *percentage* of people you need to hear from goes *down* as the population size goes *up*. This is because there are only so many opinions to be held in the first place. In other words, let's say we asked people if they would rather startle a porcupine, a skunk, or a rattlesnake. If we asked just ten people, we might need to ask all ten before we got a clear idea of the group's real preference because the decision (in my mind anyway) is not a happy one, and with serious consequences to boot. But let's say you wanted to poll five thousand people on the same question. Assuming that a trend would develop, you would not have to talk to all five thousand. You might recognize a pattern after just a few hundred or certainly after a couple of thousand. So percentage-wise, you had to ask close to 100 percent of the group of ten, but probably somewhere less than 50 percent of the big group. If you were asking one hundred thousand people, you might only need to collect opinions from 2–3 percent before you could figure out how things were going. (And by the way, I will take my chances on the porcupine—I think they are less reactive— just my personal opinion.)

The other two issues, margin of error and specificity, are best handled together in this discussion. When we talk about margin of error, we are talking about our estimates of the proportion of the population who respond one way or another. In our example above, maybe the breakdown would look like this:

Porcupine preference	40%
Skunk preference	35%
Rattlesnake preference	25%

Although that looks fine, and very specific, remember we did not hear from *everyone*. That means that we could be off in our estimates. We don't want to make too many mistakes when we report survey results, so we have to hedge our statements just a little to be reasonably sure we are correct in what we are saying. This is best done by expanding our estimates a little:

Porcupine preference	38–42%
Skunk preference	33–37%
Rattlesnake preference	23--27%

By reporting like that, we are more likely to have reported the true percentage than if we had attempted to be spot-on precise with a number. If you think about it, the wider the range we use, the more certain we can be that we are correct. In fact, I can tell you with absolute certainty, without even doing a poll, that the following preferences, when stated, are true:

Porcupine preference	0-100%
Skunk preference	0-100%
Rattlesnake preference	0-100%

Of course that doesn't help answer the question much to know that somewhere between nobody and everybody, some percent would prefer to startle a porcupine (or skunk or rattlesnake). We are in the *actionable* information business. We have to do some better than that wide range. Therefore, there is now another decision to be made whenever we want to know how many people to talk to — how specific do we have to be in our stated results?

The final consideration is already implied. We need actionable information to be somewhat precise in order to make plans. But just how important is it to be right all the time? What if the information we gave out was right 99 percent of the time? How about 95 percent of the time? Is 90 percent or even 80 percent reporting credibility enough to do the job? The fewer times we have to be correct, the more precise we can be. The more times we have to be correct, the less precise we have to be — unless we start polling more people. This reminds me of a quotation I heard attributed to the legendary oil field firefighter, "Red" Adair. He was challenged (as the story goes) by a particularly complex and hazardous oil field blaze. He reportedly told the field manager, "I can get this done for you cheap, fast, or right — pick any two." The same thing applies to survey sampling: You can be precise; you can collect a small/quick sample; you can be sure of being correct — pick any two.

For those of you who would like a quick way to estimate the numbers you need to provide you with survey results you can live with, there is a simple solution provided to you courtesy of the Internet. Just go to any major search engine that you like and type in the words, "sample size calculator." You will then be offered several sites that allow you to enter your level of confidence (typically 95 percent or 99 percent, but many will let you choose whatever you want), then put in the margin of error you can live with (plus or minus some small amount like 3, 4, or 5 percent, usually). It then will ask you for the population size (which you can estimate if you have to) and it will tell you exactly how many responses you will need to achieve the levels of precision and accuracy you are looking for. It is that easy to set a target response amount. The greater challenge is probably convincing that many people to cooperate. We will tackle that part next.

Getting Respondents Engaged Enough to Respond with Thoughtful Answers

Some people actually enjoy giving feedback on surveys and filling out assessment forms. Of course, some people enjoy vacuuming, bungee jumping, and/or viewing foreign films with English subtitles. What we have to concern ourselves with is the part of the population that doesn't derive any particular satisfaction out of responding to survey questions—probably the majority of folks, if the truth be told.

We can take a lesson from commercial advertising experts. They face a challenge not all that different from assessment and survey designers: capturing the attention of people who do not expect to care about what it is you have to say or want them to do. Yet it has become a part of national culture in the U.S. for a large percentage of viewers to tune into the Super Bowl for the express purpose of watching the commercials. People watch them primarily because they are *not* your everyday, unimaginative commercials. They manage to draw the viewers into their stories—the writers go to the trouble of designing a presentation that does not rely on relentless repetition to make its point. Capturing peoples' attention without endless repetition is exactly what an assessment or survey has to do.

How do we go about drawing people into our surveys? It is advisable to include as many of these features as you can:

- Build anticipation for the instrument by increasing awareness of the topic in general prior to its release (at meetings, via the corporate intranet or newsletter, through email, etc.).
- Win the endorsement of an influential member of the organization supporting the "cause" that the survey or assessment represents.
- Include, in your introduction to the instrument, a description of the benefit to the respondent to participate (improving something in their lives, having their voice "heard," being part of a "select" group invited to respond, etc.).
- Use online surveys whenever practical because of the greater presentation and data collection flexibility.
- Provide a variety of response mechanisms (mix up radio buttons, drop down lists, check boxes, fill in the blanks, etc.).

- Allow them to see their progress with task-bar completion thermometers or pop-up messages cheering respondents onward.
- Include (when appropriate) humor and surprises in the layout or items themselves; insert references to porcupines whenever possible (this last part was an example of a clever humor surprise, see?).
- If appropriate, allow for respondents to see a summary of their responses as compared to the responses of the entire responding population; people like to see how they "stacked up" relative to others.
- Color, layout, and animation when carefully presented will enhance and engage without becoming a distraction.

If you are able to include most of these features in the administration of your instruments, you will find that people are going to be willing to complete the forms. The effort then becomes to keep them engaged in answering the items thoughtfully.

Keeping Respondents Attentive

The reader has to be sufficiently engaged to really read and *consider* what is being asked in order to give a thoughtful answer. If, for example, the wording is repetitive and if the same response sets are always being provided in the same order, the respondent will start to become lulled into a kind of hypnotic trance. We experience this same type of effect if we spend an extended period driving along a lightly traveled highway or turnpike that has limited visual interest. Have you ever been driving along, only to suddenly realize you are at (or even past) your desired exit? It is because your brain has experienced the same limited inputs for so long that you tend to lapse into a sort of "autopilot" mode and start thinking of other things. Even though this condition is potentially serious when you are driving, it happens all the time, and so it is easy to imagine how a monotonous set of assessment questions could lull us into the same mind-numbness. We must keep respondent attention and focus on our survey items if we hope to receive good information.

Let's continue to consider how our minds work. The first aspect is the hypnotic effect of repetitive items. The second process I will label "recall/reaction chunking." By that, I mean our feelings and opinions are the aggregation of a number of "mini-reactions" to minor events that we don't consciously remember, particularly if the experience overall was somewhat neutral. Remember our *Coûteux Nourriture* restaurant example from chapter 2? Two examples were given: one of a really nice dining experience and one of a fairly bad experience. But what if the experience was just mildly pleasant? In a case like that, we would not typically recall having memorable reactions to the quality of each of the food items, to the speed of the service, to insignificant verbal exchanges with the staff, and so forth and so on. When the experience is of the "okay to good" variety, we "chunk" our reactions and recollection of the event. Certainly if we had an exceptionally great experience or an exceptionally terrible experience, we could vividly recall specific elements. In the grand scheme of life, these extreme experiences don't seem to happen much. This is a critical concept.

Critical Concept Alert!
Most experiences from which we form opinions are not memorable enough for us to be able to give a detailed and thoughtful response. At best, we have an "overall' reaction.

This concept has several significant ramifications. Assume that you are rating a common experience that is largely unremarkable. There is a good chance that the following things could happen:

• If asked *too many detailed rating questions* about which you do not recall a particular reaction, you will tend to default to a mildly positive response (sometimes called acquiescence bias) that may or may not reflect reality. For example, assume you are being asked to rate your experience with an average call into a customer service center. . .

o How would you rate the speed by which your call was answered?

☐	☐	☐	☐	☐
Very slow	Somewhat slow	About average	Somewhat quickly	Fast

o How would you rate the representative's tone of voice?

☐	☐	☐	☐	☐
Rude & cold	Mildly negative	Neutral	Somewhat friendly	Warm & kind

• If presented with fixed response answers that call for *a greater level of reaction* than the stimulus (the query item) produces, you will tend to default to a mildly positive or neutral response. Thinking about that unremarkable customer service call again . . .

- o Regarding the *volume* of the customer service rep's voice, would you describe it as:

☐	☐	☐	☐	☐
So soft as to be barely audible	Soft but audible	Normal	Loud & clear	Deafening

- If the response mechanism calls for a *numeric quantification of an emotional or sensory response*, an effect I describe as "survey fatigue" sets in rapidly. This results in the "default" response described above for the bulk of the rest of the items. As an illustration, only three questions are included, but there is a good chance you will find them tiring:
  - o On a scale from 1–10, with 10 being as happy as you can imagine, how happy were you overall last week?
  - o On a scale from 1–10, with 10 being terrified to the point of suffering post-traumatic stress syndrome, how frightening was the spookiest part of the last horror movie you saw?
  - o On a scale from 1–10, with 10 being the softest thing you have ever felt, how soft is your bedroom pillow?

It is important that I emphasize we are referring to the *bulk* of human experiences—the experiences that do not cause us to have an extreme reaction—the ones that leave no distinct impressions on us. In most cases, that is 80 percent (roughly) of life's daily experiences. If we were to be referring to that significant 20 percent, then many of these rules would not apply.

> It is hard for me to imagine that there are more than 20 percent of people who give a lot of thought to porcupine appearance or temperament.

Considering that probably 20 percent or less of life's experiences produce profound effects on us emotionally, wouldn't it be great if we could get feedback from only the group that had a profound reaction to whatever we were inquiring about (the 20 percent)? That is the Holy Grail. We need to figure out ways to design surveys and assessments that account for (or eliminate) the portion of the population that is having that standard, "80 percent" reaction to whatever we are asking about. At the same time, we have to capture the "good" data from the 20 percent that are passionate about an issue.

What makes the "passionate" 20 percent so important when we need actionable information? This is the group that can either identify the major positives (strengths) of an experience, or the group that can tell you what has gone sideways so you can fix the problem. For example, assume you are a porcupine breeder who wants to be known as the "Parent of Quality Porcupines" and even recognized by the IFPE.[34] It is hard for me to imagine that

---

[34] "International Federation of Porcupine Enthusiasts," a completely fictitious organization but one that I would heartily support if created.

there are more than 20 percent of people who give a lot of thought to porcupine appearance or temperament. Yet if there were to be standards of beauty and personality developed, it would be important that we knew all that we could about those standards. Are we going to hear clear and consistent opinions from the majority? Of course not! But if we could cull out the enthusiasts who had strong reactions to quill length and color, overall carriage, and personality issues, we could start setting some breeding standards. We could (with intention) affect the evolution of preferred porcupines. The same reasoning applies to more practical endeavors, like improving leadership skills or customer service. The potential is limitless but depends on separating out those who care about the topics being assessed from those who frankly have better things to worry about, but who will nevertheless offer opinions just to be polite. There has always been a tendency to end up with the two data sets mixed together, causing a lot of valuable information to be lost or diluted — until now.

Section 1: A Design that Works

This section is so-o-o exciting and so-o-o important that I am dividing it into two (count 'em: TWO) sections so you will be able to digest the information more easily. This first section will address the task of keeping respondents engaged sufficiently to consider their responses, along with providing a means by which you can cull out the useable information from the middle-of-the-road responses that tell you virtually nothing. It also provides you with a method of collecting data that requires no special software. The elegance of this approach is that it is intuitive while being sophisticated, so prepare yourself to slap your forehead and say, "Now why did no one think of this *before*?"

The effort to achieve respondent engagement is as simple as asking yourself, "What's in it for them?" Every query item needs to be focused on the issue from the perspective of the reader. Strike from your repertoire of phrases *anything* that does not directly tie back to the reader. Here are some examples of traditionally worded items and effectively worded items:

Traditional Wording	Effective Wording
Rate the instructor [the course materials, the presentation, etc]	I *personally* found the instructor [materials, presentation] to be very effective [entertaining, useful, informative, etc.].
Did the speaker maintain good eye contact?	I was engaged by the speaker's effective use of eye contact; I felt she/he was talking directly to me.
How useful was the information?	I discovered several things I will put into immediate use.
Rate the learning environment	The atmosphere supported my ability to get something meaningful from the class [presentation, etc.].
Did you gain knowledge [insight, understanding, etc.]?	I personally got *at least as much* from the class [program, experience, etc.] as most of the others in attendance.

How do you rate the class overall?	I would *personally recommend* this class to others.
Was the length of the class appropriate for the amount of information covered?	I remained engaged throughout the entire session.

Of course this list could go on and on but the point of it has already been made: all items are presented as slightly positive statements—statements that a person might make to someone else if pleased with an experience. There is no requirement that the respondent consider anything except his/her personal *reaction* to the statement made. I offered examples appropriate for a training course, seminar, or speech, but the same approach can be used for reactions to customer service scenarios, evaluations of management technique, or to assess the quality of a porcupine. For example:

- I will recommend that my friends have their tires rotated at ACME Tires.
- I believe that everyone at the company would do well to model my manager's leadership techniques.
- I would be proud to claim Porcupine #12 as my own.

You see, it makes no difference what you need to have evaluated or assessed. It will work for anything that produces a reaction so long as the critical element of your statement is embedded in a "positively loaded" statement of opinion and the opinion is framed as if it were being stated by the respondent.

190

Let's review what this does:

- It keeps the focus on the individual responding more than on the topic in question.
  - Remember, people are *most interested* in what they personally think.
  - People are only certain about their own intimate *reactions* — everything else is judgment or pure speculation.
  - Statements are then considered relative to the individual just as we all process our world — the phrase, "It's all about me" has a basis in human nature.
  - If a statement is phrased as if it will be attributed to the respondent, the respondent will consider what she/he is saying carefully — people do not like others to "put words into their mouths" and will correct misstatements attributed to them.

- By keeping the statement positively loaded, there is less energy expended on "unimportant" queries.
  - Most people who have a limited reaction to something will offer a mildly positive response anyway — this gives them a comfortable point from which to react without having to think or overanalyze much — they will remain fresh and focused for longer periods.

- All statements reflect a perception of reality that is the only basis we have for any judgments we make.
  - Our only ways of collecting input is through our five senses (unless you allow for psychic input, which would make it six senses).

- o Whether we use five or six means by which we collect inputs, ultimately the inputs have to be filtered through our minds.
- o Anything that is subject to our mental processes is perception and is automatically filtered through our variable, imperfect processing; even the most objective of scientific observers knows it is wise to test and re-test and to allow others to test and re-test in order to arrive at a mutually agreed upon consensus of the result.
- o The fewer steps we require our respondents to take to confirm or deny a perception, the less chance there is of the perception being altered due to mental "over processing."

For example, the reaction to a statement is the first level (and in this case the only level) of mental activity; if a respondent is asked to "rate" in numerical fashion his or her level of *agreement,* that would be the second level of processing (because they have to decide if a "four" or a "five" or whatever was the degree of intensity felt). Then if a respondent were to be asked to "rate" a performance level *directly,* that person would then need to form an opinion, decide how balanced it was, associate it with a numeric value, then respond — this would amount to four mental processes per item. I am starting to feel tired just thinking about it. Imagine how exhausting it is for the respondent to do this ten, twenty, or fifty-plus times. After a while, they just become worn out and start marking "three" and "four" to most items to end the pain.

Now that we know how to phrase queries, we only need to decide how to set up the response mechanism. This is a straightforward effort but one that is often given entirely too little energy. The good news is that there are really only three formats (four if you include open-ended text responses) that need to be used:

1. Binary (Yes/No, Will/Won't, True/False, On/Off, etc.)
2. Degree of intensity of reaction
3. Listing applicable responses from a list
4. Text boxes for amplification of ratings where needed

Choosing which to use for any item is pretty easy. Let's consider a few positively loaded statements:

"The speaker used appropriate audience eye contact during her presentation."

In a case like this, we need to consider what reasonable boundaries are. A clue is given in the use of the word, "appropriate." People are engaged if they think they are being spoken to directly. Failure to make regular, socially acceptable eye contact diminishes the effect of the presentation. But think about it—it is possible, certainly, to make insufficient eye contact, thereby losing connection with the audience. But if we go the other way, where the speaker is making the audience members feel like they are being examined or are in a "stare down" contest, they are going to start wondering if they have gravy on their shirts or something—kind of a distraction in the opposite direction. This makes eye contact one of those characteristics that has to be "just so." Not too little or too much. This type of item is then clearly a binary response. Either the speaker got it right or not. The correct response then is "yes" or "no," not some tired scale of 1–5 or "strongly disagree/strongly agree." I have never heard anybody comment, "What wonderful eye contact the speaker had; the best I have ever enjoyed!" (As a side note, minimize your direct sustained eye contact with your pet skunk. He/she may think you are contemplating eating him/her and respond in a socially unacceptable fashion.)

"I got most everything out of the class I hoped to."

This type of sentence is more linear in terms of response options. A person could gain virtually nothing from the experience of attending a class and feel like her/his time would have been better spent back on the job or taking a nap. Maybe the experience was even unpleasant in addition to being a distraction from more useful endeavors. Perhaps the statement is true, more or less, and possibly the attendee was incredibly impressed with the insights and personal growth experienced — far beyond what had been promised or anticipated. It kind of goes from zero benefit (or even negative effects) all the way to a positive, life-affirming event that will long be remembered and applied for the betterment of humankind (like this book probably is). In this scenario, it is best to write five "anchoring" statements that guide the respondent in stating her/his reaction to the quote that is being read. The statements might be:

- I would not say this at all.
- It is stated too strongly for me.
- I would say something like this.
- I would agree but I would say it a little more strongly.
- I would be much more enthusiastic in my statement.

Another perfectly acceptable way of setting up responses would be:

- No way! The class was useless if not harmful!
- I really got very little from this class.
- That's the way I feel!
- I was impressed; I got more than I expected.
- This class did way more; I found it positively life-altering!

This type of response set requires more work on the part of the designer but has the advantage of keeping the reader more fully engaged. It is important to keep the intensity of the statements about "equally spaced" emotionally. This can be achieved if several readers discuss the wording and reach a consensus about each response option. It takes longer, but it results in good data.

"Some of the behavior changes I will be making because of the training include (mark all that apply):"
This is an excellent way to gather a number of responses in a short time. If you are looking for several reactions all related to the same topic, this is a good way to do it while keeping the number of items limited. The wording of the response options should be in that "middle ground," represented by slightly positively loaded statements unless you are identifying only extreme reactions (for marketing purposes or whatever). What is lost is the intensity of respondent reaction—but survey assessment length (and therefore respondent time) is saved in exchange for loss of detail. There is a tendency of many designers to want to list every possible response

they can think of in order to present a comprehensive list of options. I tend to choose a less aggressive option and list only those things my client is really interested in knowing about. Either approach requires that an "Other (please describe)" option be provided (in most cases, anyway). I figure that offering too many choices results in respondent fatigue and ultimately in a collection of extraneous information. Take the statement above, for example. If the desired outcomes include four big predictors of management success, we would do well to focus on those four.

☐ I will be willing to take moderate risks if there is significant gain possible.
☐ I will take the initiative to do things that need to be done without being asked.
☐ I will lead by example.
☐ I will improve my skill at expressing visions and concepts in a way that creates enthusiasm.
Other (please describe):

You know and I know that there is more to guaranteeing management success than those four behaviors. However, if those are the behaviors that the training was supposed to improve (or if those behaviors were the only ones your client is really interested in knowing about), it doesn't do much good to list a bunch of others. The more responses you obtain, the more work it is to track or summarize them. I say keep it simple.

Section 2: Taking a Design
That Works to a Whole New Level

Here it is. I saved this section for last because it is reserved for only those of you who really, really want to capture the best data possible. It is not easy to set up on your own, even though I will tell you how it works. The smart professional saves much time and aggravation by simply contacting me and having my company do it for you. But whether you choose to design your own (kind of like *building* your own jumbo jet to fly between Miami and JFK) or use my services (kind of like buying a *ticket* for the flight between Miami and JFK), you should at least understand the technology behind it. Are you ready? I hope so, because this is very cool stuff.

Theory #1: Opinions are normally distributed

What this means is that if you were to ask a huge sample of people about most anything calling for an opinion,[35] and you were able to assign a value of, say, 1–10 to the opinions they expressed, most of the opinions you would get would be in the middle range. If they were not in the middle range exactly, they would still clump up at some point. It might look like this:

---

[35] By "most anything," I mean those issues where there is a good likelihood that reasonable people might have widely varying opinions. Issues of cannibalism, genocide, or cruelty to porcupines are examples of unsuitable topics because of almost universal condemnation that would have very narrow (leptocurtic) distribution curves.

Item: "I like cats."

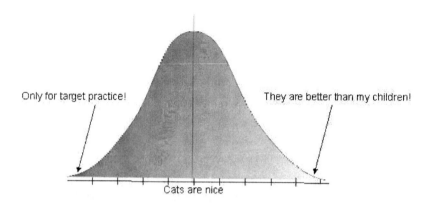

What this means is that the majority of people are of the lukewarm opinion that cats are sort of okay, more or less. Believe it or not, this is a fairly polarizing statement because many people have strongly held opinions about cats. Nevertheless, a distribution of responses would most likely look kind of like this example. This means that for all intents and purposes, somewhere around 70–80 percent of people are mildly fond of or at least able to tolerate cats. This means that 70–80 percent don't have anything intriguing to say about why cats are good or bad. If you were designing a better cat, their opinions would be of little help. Let's look at what the graph would look like if we took out that 70–80 percent:

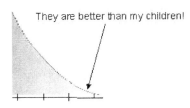

Only for target practice!

They are better than my children!

Cats are nice

Now if we were to get more detailed opinions from people at either end of that curve, we would be seeing some pretty clear ideas about what is right and what is wrong with cats, and you can bet that this portion of the sample would have some very strong suggestions and ideas.

The trick then becomes managing to collect information from these two polarized groups and forgetting the rest of the people who have wussy opinions. There are a couple of steps that help in that process. They are as follow:

- Get rid of the rating numbers (that is, remove the one-to-ten labels from the vertical grid lines).
- Encourage people to give a mid-range response; we only want the "true believers" to tell us anything. They are the only ones who really care.
- Make the response mechanism entertaining enough to keep the respondents engaged.

Here is how to do it:
- First, squish down the curve so it is flat, thereby stre-e-e-etching out the base of the curve.

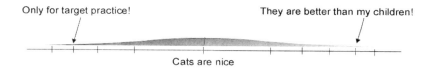

- Take the little grid lines (and numbers if you had them) away from the bottom of the distribution curve but leave verbal anchors at the ends and at the center.

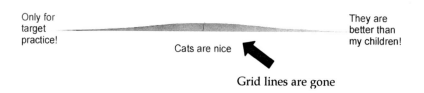

Grid lines are gone

- Now if you can imagine us looking at the squished curve from the TOP rather than straight ahead, the top of the curve might look like a ribbon. Let's mentally rotate the curve around so we are looking at it from the top:

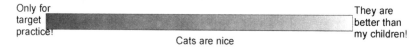

- Remember, this is in an electronic format, which means we can move a mouse pointer over the ribbon we created—this also means we can slide a vertical line right and left if we want to. It might look like this:

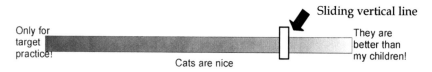

200

- Or this:

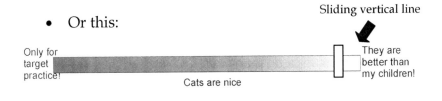

- Or this:

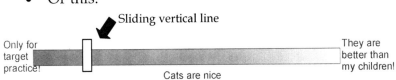

- One last step—let's make a text box appear whenever somebody slides the vertical line real far left or right, which indicates a strong positive or negative opinion about cats (here is a close-up).

Let's review what we have done:
- We took a straight line and removed the tick marks and numbers but added anchors of meaning to the line.
- We then stretched out the line to make the distribution curve almost flat, and spread out the response points so that most middle of the road responses

201

(about 80 percent of them) were easily captured in the middle.

- We converted the stretched-out grid line into a shaded box and made it possible to create an analog "slider" on the box so that people could mark exactly how strongly they felt about the statement.
- When the slider was moved far to the left or the right, a text box appeared to capture the reasoning for the extreme responses—middle of the road responses were essentially ignored.
- We then captured only the extreme positive and negative comments to find out why those people who really cared about the statement felt as they did.

This all serves the critical needs we started talking about:

- People do not have to assign numbers to feelings.
- They can be as precise (graphically) as they want to—they do not have to respond to a number or a statement that possibly does not match exactly what they are feeling.
- It is an engaging way of answering—kind of like playing a video game.
- There is limited mental fatigue, because their reactions and their responses all come from the right hemisphere of the brain.

WOW! What should we call this method of collecting responses? How about the Item Response Graphic System© (or the IRGS©, if you prefer)? It actually exists, it works, and it's spectacular. Remember, it is based on a variation of the normal distribution curve (a bell curve). It is a way to cause the values collected to be in the form of interval rather than ordinal numbers, because the values tend to be equidistant. Remember that concept from chapter 12? It makes it more appropriate to average the numbers or summarize them in other ways without losing the meaning of the responses. In my opinion, this is really the most effective way yet developed to capture the intensity of a person's opinion in a way that is universally understandable in a report. I have used this type of data collection device with a great many surveys across a wide variety of applications, from reactions to a basic customer service training program, to evaluations of manager behaviors, to even identifying the state of mind of people suffering from serious health conditions. The outcomes have been so effective that in combination with the right query items, the IRGS© grid has actually helped to save lives.[36]

To obtain that level of precision and accuracy, it is important to make certain that the tool is properly designed. If that is your desire, you are encouraged to contact me so we can work together on the development of your project. Just type in www.metrika-phoenix.com and I will be there – more or less. At least somebody will get you in touch with me if you ask them to. Some very nice people work

---

[36] The IRGS© was employed on an experimental basis several years ago by psychologists treating patients with potentially severe depression. The system correctly diagnosed several people who were suicidal who might have been overlooked while not incorrectly diagnosing anyone – this resulted in therapy that literally saved lives. If it can do that, it will probably be good enough for your next classroom evaluation.

at Metrika Phoenix if I do say so myself. They may not all be into porcupines that much but who is perfect, really?

Epilogue

Of course, we did not cover everything there is to know about test and survey design, administration, and reporting, but we did put a good dent in the project. If you have picked up an increased level of understanding of the science and art of psychometrics, I am very pleased—as you should be. If you are already a professional in this field, I hope I have adequately expressed some out-of-the-box thinking that may inspire you to offer some creative insights of your own into our profession. No matter who you are, if you took the time to read this book, I would love to hear from you—don't be shy. Knowledge seems to advance more quickly in an atmosphere of discourse.

The underlying theme of this book has been to increase the "humanity" of assessments in organizations. Frankly, I don't really think there is enough humanity in business. In the 1972 film, *The Godfather*, Michael Corleone said to Sonny, "It's not personal, Sonny. It's strictly business." Since that time, people everywhere seem to have found a pithy quote to sum up what was probably an American business tradition for decades. Just as anyone who has been "downsized," "right-sized," dehumanized, humiliated, intimidated, or otherwise abused in the name of "business" knows, there are few things more personal than business. There are few things in business that call for more personal courage than sharing honest reactions about what is happening there. Although this book, no matter how widely read and adopted, will not right all that is wrong with human behavior in organizations, it will at least help. In the final analysis, that is probably

worthwhile, if each of us works to improve the world —
even if just a little bit.

Appendix A

Way back in chapter 4, in a little obscure footnote, I promised that I would include some very simple ways to measure training outcomes quantitatively for those in an organization that would suffer serious withdrawal symptoms without them. For those of you who read that footnote, consider your efforts rewarded . . .

HARD NUMBERS TO MEASURE BUSINESS RESULTS OF TRAINING[37]

Effectiveness of Training

The effectiveness of training using test scores as a measurement of learning is determined by comparing post-test scores with pre-test scores and then measuring the net change per dollar spent. [38]

---

[37] I would like to acknowledge the creativity and insight of Mr. Bob Dust, founder and general manager of Gyrus Systems, Richmond, VA. It was his article, "The Myth of Training ROI" that stimulated much of my thinking about this "hard numbers approach" and from which the examples contained herein are inspired.

[38] As noted before, there are references to "cost of training," which is a difficult figure to calculate. The presumption is that whoever wants to get these kinds of numbers will collaborate with you on how to define costs to be used for your calculations.

Example 1: Effectiveness Skill Cost
- Pre-Post score shift average: 10 points
- Number of participants: 500
- Cost of training: $20,000

Formula:
- 500 X 10 = 5,000 point "gain"
- 20000 / 5000 = $4/point

Improvement Achieved by:
- Raise average score difference
- Reduce cost per head of training

Example 2: Effectiveness Outcome Cost
- Pre-test 175 participants had "qualifying score"
- Post-test 300 total participants had "qualifying score"
- Number of participants: 500
- Cost of training: $20,000

Formula:
- 300 – 175 = 125 qualifiers from training
- 20000 / 125 = $160 / new qualified trainee

Improvement Achieved by:
- Reduce or eliminate those with qualifying scores on pre-class test thereby reducing total training cost (in this case, had there been a straight-line reduction in cost for less participants, the total cost would have been $13,000, resulting in a cost of $104 / new qualified trainee)

Efficiency of Training

The efficiency of training shows how much training was delivered per some unit, for example, the cost per participant hour of training delivered. A full classroom is more efficient than one that is half full.

Example 3: Training Efficiency
Cost/participant hour
- 10-hour course costs $20,000
- 10 participants

Formula:
- 20000/10 = $2,000/hr
- 2000/10 = **$200**/participant hour

Improvement Achieved by:
Increasing headcount per course (See Example 4)

Example 4: Training Efficiency
Cost/participant hour
- 10-hour course costs $20,000
- 20 participants

Formula:
- 20000/10 = $2,000/hr
- 2000/20 = **$100**/participant hour

Improvement Achieved by:
Increasing headcount per course (50% cost efficiency improvement over Example 3)

Comparing Effectiveness to Efficiency

Notice that the effectiveness metrics focus on quality, and the efficiency metrics focus on quantity. Your training is moving in the right direction if your effectiveness costs are going down and your efficiency ratios are going up.

Effectiveness and efficiency are noble and honorable metrics, but they ignore the demand for training and the business reasons for doing the training. The next two metrics address those concerns.

Applicability Ratio

The applicability ratio shows how the training is aligned with the business objectives. What good is raising employee skill ratings and putting more employees through training if the organization does not need those skills? The applicability ratio is a simple calculation, but it is rather difficult to gather the supporting data.

To calculate the applicability ratio, divide those training costs that are identified for specific skills in "demand" by the organization, by the total for all training costs. This can be done for a particular course or for the entire training operation. The "demand" can be based on whatever criteria you choose. It can be determined from a needs-analysis survey of employees, based on learning objectives and program content, executive leadership determination based on strategic objectives, etc. The course must somehow be defined as "mission critical" or "non mission-critical" with the advise and consent of stakeholders.

Example 5: Applicability Ratio
- 5 courses offered
- 3 mission-critical
- Cost per student/course is $1,000
- 60 employees take mission-critical courses
- 20 employees take non mission-critical courses

Formula:
- 60 + 20 = 80 participants
- 60/80 = .75 = 75%
- 80 X 1000 = $80,000 spent
- 75% of total expenditures ($60K) was spent on mission critical training

---

Appropriateness Ratio

The appropriateness ratio shows that the right learning objects are delivered to the right people. Having excellent training is wasted if you are teaching computer programmers how to sell, or if you are teaching social workers how to program computers. It is similar to the applicability ratio, but provides more accountability by measuring the training of the specific people assigned to specific business objectives. Such training can be linked by job function, project, team, or business objective.

To calculate the appropriateness ratio, divide the training costs for training those people identified with specific business objectives by the total cost of all training.

Example 6: Appropriateness Ratio
- 10 skill-specific courses are offered
- Cost per person per course is $2000
- 150 people enroll in the courses
- 50 people are tagged as "skill required" attendees (need program to meet organizational objectives)

Formula:
- 150 X 2000 = $300,000 training cost
- 50 / 150 = .33 = 33% of attendees were skill required
  (Appropriateness ratio = 33%)
- 300000 X .33 = $100,000 of training was skill required

Improvement Achieved by:
Giving priority (or restricting availability to) "skill-required" attendees.

Of course, these measures, like any purely objective quantifiable measures, are somewhat deficient in identifying or reflecting the more "intangible" but nevertheless significant aspects of organizational development. A drive simply to optimize ratios such as these would likely be at the expense of other factors like morale, commitment, and job satisfaction. Those factors could in turn affect other business metrics like turnover, productivity, and profitability.

As always, a blend of approaches tempered by common sense and humanity is still the best overall strategy.

Appendix B

Just as the manuscript was in the final stages of editing, one of my proofreaders suggested that it would be nice if we reprinted those little pearls that I call Generally Unacknowledged Measurement Principles.

Being the overachiever I am, I not only have included the Generally Unacknowledged Measurement Principles here but have thrown in the six Scaling Rules and a Critical Concept Alert.

So much value in so few pages — wow.

Generally Unacknowledged Measurement Principle #1:
Any measurement or rating system, no matter how perfectly constructed, can be rendered worthless in the hands of an incompetent rater. Conclusions drawn from such administrations are therefore invalid.

Generally Unacknowledged Measurement Principle #2:
If the precision of a measurement tool exceeds the user's capabilities to recognize and differentiate between measurement points, the points themselves are rendered ineffective and inaccurate. This in turn produces results that are incorrect and misleading.

Generally Unacknowledged Measurement Principle #3:
The accuracy and validity of conclusions drawn from a convenience sample are inversely proportional to the relative variability.

Generally Unacknowledged Measurement Principle #4:
The smaller the population of interest, the larger the proportion of the population you must sample.

Generally Unacknowledged Measurement Principle #5:
If you want measurement to influence the outcome of the process you are measuring positively, you need to measure outcomes during the event process. Only current and timely measurements provide completely actionable information.

Generally Unacknowledged Measurement Principle #6:
Most people feel they have better things to do than to answer questions. However, most people also think they are smarter than you. If asked properly, they will tell you all about themselves and their world in hopes of impressing you with their insight and wisdom.

Generally Unacknowledged Measurement Principle #7:
It doesn't make much difference how you word your items if they are structurally sound and have appropriate response mechanisms associated with them.

Scaling Rule #1
If you are attempting to determine if something IS or IS NOT a true condition, allow for a binary response.

Scaling Rule #2
A Likert Scale can be used for collecting a "grouping" of opinions about a general topic. It is not good to use that type of scale if you are eliciting an opinion of a single topic.

Scaling Rule #3
Scaling systems that use Likert-like scale values should NEVER be averaged together. They are best counted and presented in a chart or table.

Scaling Rule #4
If you want to be able to compute averages, standard deviations, and other more sophisticated analyses, you have to use rational or interval data. Only a few scaling systems can provide that type of data, though—be careful!

Scaling Rule #5
For most scaling approaches, consider carefully including "escape" responses such as "Other," "None," "Does not apply," "I don't know," "I choose not to respond," etc. to prevent unintentional distortion of data.

Scaling Rule #6
No matter how good a system you have for collecting data, there is some advantage to picking up some qualitative information along the way. It is cumbersome to work with, but usually adds clarity and depth to your analysis.

Critical Concept Alert!
Most experiences from which we form opinions are not memorable enough for us to be able to give a detailed and thoughtful response. At best, we have an "overall' reaction.

Index

Representative sample, 17, 25, 26, 27, 28, 175, 175,

response rate, 79, 81, 86, 90, 125, 140, 147, 175, 177

right brain, 89, 137

right hemisphere, 89, 137, 202

ROI, iv, 44, 45, 47, 48, 49, 50, 52, 102, 116, See Chapter 4

sample size calculator, 181

Scaling Rule #1, 160, 214

Scaling Rule #2, 163, 214

Scaling Rule #3, 168, 215

Scaling Rule #4, 169, 215

Scaling Rule #5,171, 215

Scaling Rule #6, 172, 215

Scatter Chart, 153, 154, 155

"smile" or "smiley" sheets, 79, 102, 116,

Stakeholders, 36, 37, 39, 41, 43, 47, 117, 129, 131, 132, 147, 150, 151, 152, 171, 210

Stanley Davis, i

Statistical Process Control, 72

Survey fatigue, 59, 104, 186

Theorem of Imperceptible Difference, 22, 23

"The Third Wave", ii, iii

training ROI, 44, 45, 47, 48, 49, 50, 52, 102, 116, 207

"try", "tries", "trying", "tried", These words do not appear in this book.

Uncertainty Principle, 55, 61, 67, 68, 115

Velcro, 31

W. Edwards Deming, 72

Walt Disney, 31

Walter A. Shewhart, 72

Warren Buffet, 69

Werner Heisenberg, 55, 61, 68

Printed in the United States
122980LV00001B/196-288/P